PROPERTY CRIME IN CANADA
AN ECONOMETRIC STUDY

Kenneth L. Avio and C. Scott Clark

Property Crime in Canada: an econometric study

PUBLISHED FOR THE ONTARIO ECONOMIC COUNCIL BY
UNIVERSITY OF TORONTO PRESS
TORONTO AND BUFFALO

© Ontario Economic Council 1976
Reprinted 2014
ISBN 978-0-8020-3334-5 (paper)

Library of Congress Cataloging in Publication Data

Avio, Kenneth L   1942 -
Property crime in Canada.

(Ontario Economic Council research studies; 2)
Bibliography: p.
1. Offenses against property — Canada — Mathematical
models. I. Clark, Cecil Scott, 1944 - joint author.
II. Title. III. Series: Ontario Economic Council. Ontario
Economic Council research studies; 2.
HV6807.A93   364.1'6'0971   76-925
ISBN 978-0-8020-3334-5 (pbk.)

Contents

vi Contents

Acknowledgments

The authors wish to express their gratitude to the Judicial Division of Statistics Canada, to the Local and Provincial Government Finance Sections of Statistics Canada, and also to the Statistics Section of the Ministry of the Solicitor General for aid in data collection. Excellent research assistance was provided by Susan Kirby and Manh Nguyen.

This study was first presented in a seminar at the Ontario Economic Council in Toronto in August 1974. Subsequent presentations were made at the University of Victoria, Carleton University, Queen's University, and the University of Western Ontario. The authors extend their appreciation to participants in these seminars. Many helpful suggestions were provided during informal discussions with colleagues at the University of Victoria and the University of Western Ontario.

PROPERTY CRIME IN CANADA:
AN ECONOMETRIC STUDY

Introduction

This study summarizes early results of an attempt to apply an economic model of crime to explain recorded property crime rates in Canada. The model is adapted from the economic model of criminal behaviour originally proposed by Becker (1968) and later estimated in various forms, notably by Ehrlich (1973), Sjoquist (1973), and Swimmer (1974) for the United States and by Carr-Hill and Stern (1973) for England and Wales. The model includes a supply-of-offences function and a police production function for each property crime, as well as a function explaining total government expenditures on police and protection. Empirical results are presented only for the supply-of-offences functions for four different property crimes. The equations are estimated using provincial data for 1970, 1971, and 1972.

The model and empirical results reported herein differ in three major respects from previous published studies (all utilizing United States or United Kingdom data) of supply-of-offences equations. First, with one exception previous studies have explicitly assumed that prospective offenders consider only the probability of incarceration as a risk variable and do not, for example, distinguish between the risk of apprehension and the risk of conviction once apprehended. In this scheme the offender associates a zero cost to apprehension if he is not convicted, and hence pre-trial incarceration, bail costs, legal fees, and so on are implicitly removed from the offender's decision calculus. The lone exception in the published literature is found in a single estimated equation reported by Sjoquist (1973, 444, eq. 4). Aggregate property crime is the dependent variable in the equation, and the data base is a cross-section of US cities. Sjoquist found the clearance rate to have a signficant deterrent effect on the crime rate, whereas the influence of the conviction rate (conditional upon apprehension) was insignificant. Our results differ from Sjoquist's. In Canada, the probability of apprehension has a significant negative effect on recorded crime rates for break and enter, robbery and theft. The latter two crime categories are also inversely related to the conviction rate.

Second, as a proxy for the expected sentence length in a given year, most researchers have used a weighted average of sentences served by releasees in the same year, with the weights being equal to the proportion of releasees who have served a given sentence length.[1] This weighted average will not accurately represent expected sentence length if sentences change over time, and if prospective offenders are aware of these changes. Two other difficulties emerge. In appendix A we demonstrate that even if sentences do not change over time, the conventional measure of expected sentence length leads to spurious results if the number of offenders subjected to incarceration changes from period to period. In addition to this purely 'statistical' problem there is the possibility that the variable is measuring the impact of effects other than the deterrent effect, namely, 'removal' and 'training' effects (Avio, 1973). Longer sentences keep offenders isolated from legitimate society for longer periods, and longer incarcerations allow offenders more time to learn criminal and/or legitimate skills, thus affecting their proclivity to commit crime upon release. These effects preclude the interpretation of the estimated sentence length elasticity as a pure deterrent effect.[2] All conceivable proxies for expected sentence length must be suspected of partially picking up these effects, but measures relating directly to the experience of released offenders (as does the commonly used measure) are particularly suspect. As an alternative, a weighted average of sentences handed down by the courts in a given year, corrected for parole and remission possibilities, is used in this study. The generally significant inverse relation between expected sentence length and the recorded crime rate found by other researchers (cf. Tullock, 1974) is not found for any of the property crimes investigated in this study.

A third major result has implications for the interpretation of supply-of-offences functions. Although the central hypothesis of the property criminal as a utility maximizer is substantially supported by the empirical results of this

---

1 Carr-Hill and Stern (1973) used the percentage of convicted persons sent to prison as a proxy for costs associated with a prison term. This proxy has the serious deficiency that, for example, a sentence of ten years is implicitly assumed to have the same deterrent effect as a sentence of one month.

2 Ehrlich (1973) demonstrates theoretically that the existence of effects other than a pure 'removal' effect can be established. However, he has not demonstrated that the deterrent effect can be empirically distinguished from 'training' effects (cf. n.22).

study, the relative impact of the explanatory variables often depends upon the particular crime category involved. For example, the percentage of the male population between the ages of fifteen and twenty-four has a significant negative impact upon the number of robberies committed, but little effect upon the number of thefts. Results of this sort indicate that the procedure of estimating supply-of-offences functions over aggregates of crime categories (e.g. 'property' crime) may lead to unjustified generalizations about individual crime types, and in fact may invalidate such studies as a legitimate attempt to subject the economic model of crime to empirical verification. Since most published studies do use aggregate property crime as the dependent variable (e.g. Sjoquist, 1973; Carr-Hill and Stern, 1973; Greenwood and Wadycki, 1973) our results have implications for the design of future research.

This study contains six chapters. The first is an overview of the extent of property crime in Canada; the second presents the 'crime' model; the third describes the data used; the fourth provides estimates of the supply-of-offences functions; the fifth presents an illustrative example of the possible relationship between estimated and 'true' crime elasticities; and the sixth summarizes the arguments, indicates the conclusions, and makes recommendations for future research.

1

The extent of property crime in Canada

Table 1 lists recorded crimes (criminal code violations only) and crime rates for Canada and the provinces for the years 1966 and 1971. These figures give substance to the growing unease of Canadians regarding the safety of their persons and property. For Canada as a whole the total number of violations almost doubled over the five-year period. Moreover, the change in the total crime rate indicates that the increase in the number of offences was not due primarily to the increase in population.

Crime in Canada during the period was not evenly dispersed among the provinces. In 1966 British Columbia had the highest total crime rate (Yukon and Northwest Territories excluded) in Canada, followed by the other western provinces. The total crime rates in Quebec and New Brunswick (the provinces with the lowest crime rates in 1966) were less than one-half British Columbia's total crime rate. By 1971 the differential between the regions had for the most part increased. Manitoba, Alberta, and British Columbia all experienced increases in their total crime rates of over 50 per cent, whereas in the Atlantic provinces the largest increase occurred in Nova Scotia, about 24 per cent. Ontario had the largest percentage increase in the total crime rate over the period, 64 per cent; by 1971 Ontario had replaced Saskatchewan as the fourth-ranked province in crime rates.

Possibly some of the increase in the national and provincial recorded crime rates is purely 'statistical' and attributable to several factors. Statistics Canada's Uniform Crime Reporting System undoubtedly has improved not only in coverage but also in recording technique. The police may be becoming more efficient in detecting crime as the quantity and quality of manpower and capital

TABLE 1

Reported crime and crime rates by province

	1966						1971					
	Crimes against persons		Crimes against property		Total		Crimes against persons		Crimes against property		Total	
Province	Number	Rate	Number	Rate	Number	Rate	Number	Rate	Number	Rate	Number	Rate
Newfoundland	1,692	3.4	10,340	20.9	12,032	24.3	1,930	3.6	13,313	25.4	15,243	29.1
Prince Edward Island	510	4.6	2,563	23.6	3,073	28.3	325	2.9	2,086	18.6	2,411	21.6
Nova Scotia	3,093	4.0	13,080	17.3	16,173	21.3	3,327	4.2	17,578	22.2	20,905	26.4
New Brunswick	1,981	3.2	10,363	16.8	12,344	20.0	1,922	3.0	12,518	19.7	14,440	22.7
Quebec	11,014	1.9	105,728	18.2	116,742	20.1	13,426	2.2	161,446	26.7	174,872	29.0
Ontario	23,458	3.3	171,888	24.6	195,346	28.0	41,114	5.3	313,920	40.7	355,034	46.0
Manitoba	2,498	2.5	27,918	28.9	30,416	31.5	3,708	3.7	43,587	44.1	47,295	47.8
Saskatchewan	3,968	4.1	25,503	26.6	29,471	30.8	4,824	5.2	35,044	37.8	39,868	43.0
Alberta	7,339	5.0	44,792	30.6	52,131	35.6	10,990	6.7	80,750	49.6	91,740	56.3
British Columbia	11,393	6.0	69,159	36.9	80,452	42.9	13,564	6.2	128,614	58.8	142,178	65.0
Yukon and Northwest Territories	3,064	71.1	6,715	155.8	9,779	226.9	1,726	32.4	3,762	70.7	5,488	103.1
CANADA	69,910	3.5	487,818	24.4	557,959	27.9	96,856	4.5	812,618	37.7	909,474	42.2

NOTE: Crimes against persons includes murder, attempted murder, manslaughter, rape, other sexual offences, woundings, and assaults; Crimes against property includes robbery, breaking and entering, theft of motor vehicles, theft, possession of stolen goods, and frauds; Rate means number of offences per thousand population; certain crimes, such as prostitution, are omitted from the totals of crimes against persons and property.
SOURCE: *Crime Statistics*, 1966, 1971, Statistics Canada, Cat. 85-205

inputs increases, and they may be devoting more resources to the processing of data on crime. Finally, the public may be becoming more willing to report crime. However, the relatively short time span involved in Table 1 casts doubt upon attributing the entire increase in recorded crime rates to factors independent of changes in the actual crime rates.

A direct inference from Table 1 is the relative importance of crimes that yield a monetary gain to the offender, that is, crimes against property. For Canada, property crimes outnumbered person crimes by approximately seven to one in 1966 and eight to one in 1971. The same pattern is true at the provincial level, although there are substantial differences between provinces. For the Atlantic provinces in 1966 the ratio of property crimes to person crimes ranged from four to one in the case of Nova Scotia to six to one in Newfoundland. By 1971 property crime had increased in relative importance in each of the Atlantic provinces. For Quebec, the ratio of property crimes to person crimes increased from approximately ten to one in 1966 to twelve to one in 1971, the latter being the highest ratio among all provinces in 1971. Ontario and Manitoba were the only provinces in which the ratio of property crimes to person crimes remained relatively constant over the five-year period. For Ontario this ratio was approximately eight to one and for Manitoba twelve to one. In Saskatchewan, Alberta, and British Columbia property crimes outnumbered person crimes by almost six to one in 1966. By 1971 this ratio had increased to about seven to one in Saskatchewan and Alberta and to over nine to one in British Columbia. These figures indicate not only that property crimes are more pervasive than crimes against the person but also that they are growing at a faster rate in each of the provinces. These facts indicate the need for a study devoted exclusively to the causes of property crimes.

The number of crimes may not accurately reflect the harm done to society as a result of criminality.[3] A more exact measure of social damages is the sum of 1/ lost legitimate output due to the participation of labour and capital inputs in illegal endeavours, 2/ private expenditures on crime prevention, including physical protection devices such as burglar alarms, insurance against loss risks, and the value of personal time devoted to protection, 3/ the destruction of assets, including the loss of human capital in cases of crimes against the person, and 4/ the cost of apprehending, convicting, and correcting offenders (i.e. the

---

3 For example, it is widely believed that the actual number of marijuana violations increased dramatically in the late 1960s. However, the police and the courts exercised leniency in the prosecution of violaters and in the sentences given to convicted offenders. Thus, the increase in the expenditures of the criminal justice system (one component of the true social cost of crime) was not commensurate with the increase in the number of crimes committed.

TABLE 2

Consolidated government expenditures for protection of persons and property
(excluding national defence)

Type	1966		1971	
	Amount ($ millions)	Percentage of total government expenditure	Amount ($ millions)	Percentage of total government expenditure
Courts of law			161.4	0.4
Correctional services			209.4	0.6
Police services			646.9	1.8
Firefighting services			239.1	0.7
Regulatory services			162.0	0.4
Others			84.1	0.2
Total	841.1	4.4	1502.9	4.1

NOTE: Breakdown of expenditures not available in 1966
SOURCE: *Consolidated Government Finance,* 1966, 1971, Statistics Canada, Cat. 68-202

costs of the criminal justice system). These are usually referred to by economists as the 'social costs of crime.'[4]

Unfortunately, reliable estimates of some of these components do not exist. Most of us lock and unlock doors several times a day, for example, and it would be impossible to obtain a reliable estimate of the value of time spent in this activity, or even of time expended on the protection of personal property in general. Expenditures on the criminal justice system are the social cost least difficult to examine.

Table 2 lists consolidated government expenditures by all levels of government for the protection of persons and property for 1966 and 1971 (national defence expenditures excluded). In 1971 well over one and one-half billion dollars were expended on the protection of persons and property by all levels of government combined. These expenditures represented a 71 per cent increase over those in 1966, although the fraction of government resources devoted to this category of expenditure declined slightly over the interval, from 4.4 to 4.1

4 Note that for certain crimes such as theft the loss to the victim per se is not considered a social loss – it is simply a transfer from one member of society (the victim) to another (the offender). However, under certain conditions (e.g. a perfectly competitive labour supply of offenders), the loss to the victim may approximate the value of resources used in committing the criminal act, and hence, may be included as a proxy for resource costs.

TABLE 3

Consolidated expenditures of provincial and municipal governments for the protection of persons and property, $ millions

Province	1966			1971				
	Expenditure on protection	Total government expenditure	Protection as percentage of total	Expenditure on protection	Percentage change in protection expenditure 1966-71	Total government expenditure	Percentage change in total expenditure 1966-71	Protection as percentage of total
Newfoundland	6.7	280.9	2.4	12.5	86.6	581.3	106.9	2.2
Prince Edward Island	1.4	53.3	2.6	2.3	64.3	112.2	110.5	2.0
Nova Scotia	15.2	331.3	4.6	29.0	90.8	707.4	113.5	4.1
New Brunswick	11.2	270.0	4.1	22.3	99.1	554.2	105.3	4.0
Quebec	180.7	2,961.7	6.1	326.2	80.5	6,343.4	114.2	5.1
Ontario	256.6	3,803.0	6.7	502.1	95.7	8,407.5	121.1	6.0
Manitoba	27.3	460.2	5.9	45.5	66.7	927.1	101.5	4.9
Saskatchewan	23.9	529.0	4.5	35.2	47.3	841.2	59.0	4.2
Alberta	60.0	927.6	6.5	110.2	83.7	1,898.5	104.7	5.8
British Columbia	67.5	977.6	6.9	119.0	76.3	2,152.2	120.2	5.5
Yukon and Northwest Territories	1.7	21.2	8.0	6.2	265.0	121.3	472.2	5.1

NOTE: Provincial-local transfers have been eliminated
SOURCE: *Consolidated Government Finance*, 1966, 1971, Statistics Canada, Cat. 68-202

TABLE 4

Consolidated expenditures of provincial and municipal governments in selected areas, 1971, $ millions

Province	(1) Natural resources	(2) Environment	(3) Recreation and culture	(4) Protection
Newfoundland	13.6	24.9	7.9	12.5
Prince Edward Island	1.6	1.8	2.5	2.3
Nova Scotia	7.7	25.4	9.3	29.0
New Brunswick	16.0	13.5	11.5	22.3
Quebec	69.8	167.7	151.9	326.2
Ontario	84.4	269.3	235.3	502.1
Manitoba	26.0	35.7	41.5	45.5
Saskatchewan	20.9	18.7	16.1	35.2
Alberta	39.6	62.4	50.9	110.2
British Columbia	82.7	82.9	78.6	119.0
Yukon and Northwest Territories	0.9	4.7	2.3	6.2

NOTE: Provincial-local transfers have been eliminated. Natural Resources include fish and game, forests, mines, oil and gas and water power; Environment includes water purification and supply, sewage collection and disposal, garbage and waste collection and disposal, and pollution control.
SOURCE: *Consolidated Government Finance*, 1971, Statistics Canada, Cat. 68-202

per cent. In Table 3 the consolidated expenditures of provincial and municipal governments for the protection of persons and property in 1966 and in 1971 are summarized by province. Excluding the Yukon and Northwest Territories, New Brunswick exhibited the largest percentage increase in protection expenditures over the five-year period, 99.1 per cent, and Saskatchewan the lowest, only 47.3 per cent. In every province, however, the relative share of expenditures on protection declined. Despite the declines this category of government expenditure remained large relative to many other categories. As a comparison, provincial and municipal government expenditures in 1971 on environment, natural resources, recreation and culture, and protection are listed in Table 4. Expenditures for protection of persons and property exceeded expenditures on each of the three categories listed in Table 4, except for Newfoundland's expenditures on natural resources and environment and Prince Edward Island's expenditures on recreation and culture.

Both absolutely and relatively (to other uses of funds) expenditure on the criminal justice system seems so large that an efficient allocation of resources is not an unimportant question. Table 5 provides a breakdown of provincial and municipal government expenditures on crime control in 1971. For all provinces

TABLE 5

Consolidated expenditures of provincial and local governments on crime control, 1971

Province	Courts of law ($ M)	Correctional services ($ M)	Police services ($ M)	Total ($ M)	Courts of law (%)	Correctional services (%)	Police services (%)
Newfoundland	0.9	1.9	5.0	7.8	11.5	24.4	64.1
Prince Edward Island	0.3	0.2	1.0	1.5	20.0	13.3	66.7
Nova Scotia	3.8	3.4	9.3	16.5	23.0	20.6	56.4
New Brunswick	2.2	1.9	7.8	11.9	18.5	16.0	65.6
Quebec	43.5	18.3	154.3	216.1	20.1	8.5	71.4
Ontario	44.8	63.9	207.3	316.0	14.2	20.2	65.6
Manitoba	3.6	5.6	16.3	25.5	14.1	22.0	63.9
Saskatchewan	3.3	3.4	14.2	20.9	15.8	16.3	67.9
Alberta	16.6	12.0	34.7	63.3	26.2	19.0	54.8
British Columbia	12.8	15.7	42.1	70.6	18.1	22.2	59.6
Yukon and Northwest Territories	0.9	1.8	2.0	4.7	19.1	38.3	42.6

SOURCE: *Consolidated Government Finance,* 1971, Statistics Canada, Cat. 68-202

except the Yukon and Northwest Territories police received the largest share of expenditures, a share ranging roughly between 55 and 70 per cent. Whether this allocation of protection expenditures is efficient cannot be determined without first obtaining knowledge of the factors that influence crime. For example, it is impossible to determine whether the mix of expenditures on police and corrections is efficient without first knowing how prospective offenders react to the two separate deterrent effects: the probability of getting caught (police function) vis-a-vis the length of the sentence if convicted (judicial function). A major effort to determine the causal variables in the crime equation is therefore warranted.

2

The economic model of crime

This chapter contains a non-technical discussion of the basic economic model of criminal behaviour. Variations and more detailed expositions are found elsewhere (Fleisher, 1966; Becker, 1968; Tullock, 1969; Ehrlich, 1973; Sjoquist, 1973).

All economic models of individual decision-making are based on the elementary theory of choice. It is assumed that people make allocative decisions according to certain axioms; anyone who conforms to these axioms is said to be 'rational' (Henderson and Quandt, 1971, chap. 2). These axioms imply the existence of an (expected) utility function which is simply a mathematical representation of an individual's preferences. If the axioms do not hold, the existence of such a function is questionable, and any model of crime representing the decision-making process as the maximization of expected utility is erroneous. For this reason the present study does not investigate crimes of violence such as murder and rape. It would be difficult to argue that perpetrators of violent crimes behave according to the usual set(s) of axioms.[5]

The central precept of the economic model of criminal behaviour is that individuals who engage in property crime are rational in the aforementioned sense. The individual finds it necessary to obtain income; thus, an allocative decision concerning his scarce resource 'time' (and in some instances his scarce

5 There are some crimes of violence for which the axioms underlying the economic model of crime might hold. Murders involving some form of premeditation and motivated by economic gain might be consistent with the economic model. Most murders, however, occur in the home, involve members of the same family, and seem unpremeditated.

capital resources) must be made. He wishes to allocate his time among income earning endeavours in such a way as to maximize his expected utility. The choice set is the universe of such endeavours, including, for example, common labour, thievery, and white-collar business. To the economist the reason that one person engages in common labour while another engages in breaking and entering is not because individuals adhere to different sets of axioms but rather because the expected costs and benefits differ among individuals. Thus, an economist would reject the contention that decisions are made in two steps: first, the set of income-earning endeavours is partitioned into legal and illegal; and second, choice is confined to one or the other.

The problem for the economist is to isolate the expected costs and benefits of becoming a criminal. The costs of engaging in property crime are dependent upon 1/ the forgone income that could be obtained in a legitimate occupation, 2/ the costs of being apprehended and charged by police and of appearing in court, 3/ the costs of serving a prison sentence, and 4/ the reduction in legitimate opportunities for anyone with a criminal record. Knowledge of a prospective offender's legal opportunities and sentence lengths are necessary to obtain estimates of costs.

The benefits from property crime are dependent upon the income obtained from engaging in a criminal activity. Knowledge of the stock of plunderable wealth (i.e. the victim stock) is required to determine the monetary benefits.[6]

Thus far, benefits and costs have been discussed as if they accrue with certainty. Of course, they do not. The source of uncertainty is whether or not the prospective offender will be successful. To transform certain costs and benefits into expected costs and benefits requires knowledge of the offender's subjective evaluations of the probability of apprehension, the probability of conviction given apprehension, and the expected sentence length if convicted.

Several assumptions are required in order to make this model suitable for empirical analysis. First, data on time spent on criminal activity by individuals do not exist; assuming a monotonic relationship between 'time spent' and the number of offences committed, the latter may be used as the variable of choice for a prospective offender. Second, the theory refers to decision-making by individuals, although only aggregate (across individuals) data are available, so

6 In the economic model of crime the individual is concerned not only with the monetary costs and benefits associated with legal and illegal activities but with the psychic costs and benefits as well. However, the use of aggregate data precludes the measurement of individuals' psychic variables. As a result the effects of these variables will be included in the stochastic error terms of the equations. Nevertheless, it might be possible in some cases to allow for possible psychic differences between homogeneous subgroups of the population (cf. discussion on youth variables in chapter 3).

that the well known problem of consistent aggregation exists (c.f. Tobin, 1950; Theil, 1954; Green, 1964). One condition for consistent linear aggregation is that equation coefficients are identical across individuals. This does not mean that all individuals commit crimes, because people differ in their subjective evaluations of the probabilities, their income, and so on. A further condition is required if the equations are estimated in log-linear form, as they are in this study. If the individual supply functions are assumed to be of this form and individuals are assumed to possess identical elasticities, then the aggregate function includes the geometric means of the variables. In order to use arithmetic means for estimation it must be assumed that the density function over individuals is homogenous of degree one with respect to changes in the individual values and the means (Tobin, 1950; Chow, 1957).[7]

Given the above assumptions, an aggregate supply of offences function for a community may be postulated for each of n property crimes. For any specific crime type i,

$$O_i^* = f_i \overset{(-)\ (?)}{(G_L, G_{C1},} \overset{(+)}{... G_{Ci},} \overset{(?)\ \ (?)\ \ (-)\ (?)(?)\ \ (-)\ \ (?)}{... G_{Cn}, p_1, ... p_i, ... p_n, q_1, ... q_i, ... q_n,}$$

$$\overset{(?)\ \ \ (-)\ \ (?)}{S_1, ... S_i, ... S_n, X^i), \quad (i = 1, ... n),} \quad (1)$$

where O_i^* is the actual number of offences per capita of crime type i (i.e. the 'true' crime rate); G_L is the average gain from engaging in legitimate activities (i.e. the opportunity cost of crime); $G_{C1}, ... G_{Ci}, ... G_{Cn}$ are the average gains from engaging in each of the n property crimes; $p_1, ... p_i, ... p_n$ are the average subjective probabilities of apprehension by the police for each of the n property crimes; $q_1, ... q_i, ... q_n$ are the average subjective probabilities of conviction for each of the n property crimes if the offenders are apprehended; $S_1, ... S_i, ... S_n$ are the average expected sentence lengths for the n property crimes if the offenders are convicted, and X^i is the vector of variables affecting the psychic income or 'tastes' for crime i. The sign above each variable in equation (1) indicates the predicted effect of the variable on O_i^*. Thus, an increase in the average gain from

---

7 A final condition required for unbiased estimation is that the mean value of the distribution of a variable across individuals in a community be equal to the measured value of this mean. This is a particularly strong assumption in the cases of the subjective probabilities and expected sentence length. For example, in the case of the probability of apprehension this assumption requires that the mean of the distribution of individuals' subjective probabilities of apprehension be equal to the recorded clearance rate in that community.

legitimate endeavours G_L, holding all other variables constant, should act to reduce the number of actual offences of crime type i. Note that the effects of p_j, q_j, and S_j $(j \neq i)$ are not predicted a priori, because crime categories may be complements or substitutes.[8]

Following Carr-Hill and Stern (1973) the relationship between the true and reported offence rates is emphasized here.[9] In equation (1), O_i^* refers to the actual number of crimes per capita, not necessarily the number of crimes recorded by the police. Actual and recorded offences can differ for several reasons: some offences may not be discovered; others may not be reported to the police even if they are discovered; still others may be reported to the police but not included by the police in their reports to Statistics Canada. This underrecording of the actual number of offences is referred to as the 'dark number' problem. There does not appear to be available for Canada or for individual provinces any estimates of the number of unrecorded property crimes. However, the dark number problem is likely to be less severe in the case of property crimes than in the case of victimless crimes like prostitution and violent crimes like rape, one reason being that a property crime victim cannot collect insurance if insured unless the crime is reported to the police.

The relationship between the actual crime rate and the recorded crime rate for any specific crime type i can be represented by

$$O_i = k_i (Z_1^i, Z_2^i, \dots Z_l^i) O_i^*, \quad (i = 1, \dots n), \tag{2}$$

where

$$k_i (Z_1^i, Z_2^i, \dots, Z_l^i) \leq 1$$

is a proportionality factor and the $Z_j^i, j = 1, \dots, l$, are variables that determine the ratio of recorded to total crimes. The Z_j^i, of course, may be found also on the right-hand side of equation (1). For example, if revenge motivates the reporting of crime, sentence length would be an important variable in the Z-vector.

By substituting equation (2) into equation (1) it is possible to derive a relationship between the recorded crime rate for crime type i and all other variables:

8 In addition, it is assumed that each community constitutes a self-contained market for crime. If this were not the case it would be necessary to include the relevant variables of surrounding communities. In this study, data by province are used so that this assumption is likely to hold.

9 In turn, Carr-Hill and Stern (1973, 295) acknowledge discussions with A. Goldberger on the topic.

$$O_i = g_i \overset{(?)\ (?)}{(G_L, G_{C1},} \overset{(?)}{\dots G_{Ci},} \overset{(?)\ (?)}{\dots G_{Cn}, p_1,} \overset{(?)}{\dots p_i,} \overset{(?)}{\dots p_n, q_1,} \overset{(?)\ (?)}{\dots q_i, \dots q_n,}$$

$$\overset{(?)\quad (?)\quad (?)}{S_i, \dots S_i, \dots S_n, X^i),} \quad (i = 1, \dots n). \quad (3)$$

In equation (3) the signs on the variables cannot be predicted a priori because of an 'identification' problem that arises from the previous substitution (see below).

The fourth equation in the crime model determines the recorded clearance rate for a specific crime in the community. A 'production function' for clearances of crime type i may be written as[10]

$$p_i = h_i \overset{(-)\quad (-)\quad (-)\ (-)\quad (-)\quad (?)\quad (?)\quad (?)\quad (?)}{(O_1, \dots O_i, \dots O_n, O_{PER}, O_{TRAF}, p_1, \dots p_{i-1}, p_{i+1}, \dots p_n,}$$

$$\overset{(?)\quad (+)}{p_{PER}, E),} \quad (i = 1, \dots n), \quad (4)$$

where E is expenditures per capita by police on labour and capital, O_{PER} and O_{TRAF} are crime rates for person crimes and traffic offences respectively, and p_{PER} is the recorded clearance rate associated with person crimes. The predicted signs of O_i, O_{PER} and O_{TRAF} are negative. As recorded crime rates increase, police resources are spread over more offences, with a consequent reduction in clearance rates. The effects of changes in p_j and p_{PER} on p_i ($i \neq j$) are a priori unpredictable but are included because changes in p_j or p_{PER} may induce a reallocation (of unknown direction) of police labour and capital between crime types, and hence affect p_i.

A final equation explaining expenditures on police in a community is needed to close the model. The equation is derived from society's desire for protection and is written.

$$E = m \overset{(+)\quad (+)\ (-)\quad (-)\ (-)\quad (+)\quad (+)\quad (+)}{(O_1, \dots O_n, p_1, \dots p_n, p_{PER}, O_{PER}, O_{TRAF}, B),} \quad (5)$$

where B is a measure of the tax base in a community (cf. Ehrlich, 542-3). The desire by society for protection implies that an independent increase in offence rates of any of the property crimes ($O_i, i = 1, \dots n$), person crimes (O_{PER}), or traffic offences (O_{TRAF}) should bring forth an increase in expenditure.

---

10 In equations (1) and (4) it is assumed that the mean value of the distribution of individual's subjective probabilities of apprehension can be represented by the recorded clearance rate in the community. The clearance rate is the ratio of the number of clearances to the number of reported offences. If this assumption does not hold the identification problem becomes considerably more severe (see n.12).

Recorded clearance rates for both property crimes and person crimes should have a negative effect because increases in these variables tend to reduce the public's perception of the severity of the crime problem. The ability of a community to support a police force, as reflected in the tax base B, should be positively related to the public's demand for expenditures on police.

Equations (3), (4), and (5) comprise a complete economic model of recorded property crime consisting of $2n + 1$ equations where n is the number of property crimes. The purpose of this paper is to estimate equation (3) for five different property crimes.

The identification problem resulting from the elimination of O_i^* from equation (1) will now be discussed. For purposes of estimation it is assumed that the n supply-of-offences functions are linear in the logs of all variables. Thus, the offence function for crime type i may be written

$$\ln O_i^* = \ln A_i + \sum_{j=1}^{n} a_j \ln p_j + \sum_{j=1}^{n} \beta_j \ln q_j + \sum_{j=1}^{n} \delta_j \ln S_j$$
$$+ \sum_{j=1}^{n} \gamma_j \ln G_{Cj} + \epsilon \ln G_L + \sum_{w=1}^{m} \mu_w \ln X_w^i ,$$

$$(i = 1, \dots n). \quad (6)$$

In equation (6), A_i is simply a multiplicative constant in the unlogged form of the equation, and X_w^i, $w = 1, \dots m$, are the variables in the 'tastes' vector.

Recall that the vectors $Z^i = (Z_1^i, Z_2^i, \dots, Z_l^i)$, are composed of variables that determine the extent to which actual crimes are registered by the recording agencies (i.e. by the police and Statistics Canada). The recording process is influenced by the willingness of the public to report crime and of the police to record reported crimes, and by the ability of the police (and the public) to detect crime. As mentioned above, one hypothesis is that a larger proportion of actual offences will be reported (and recorded) if the public feels that the police will be successful in apprehending offenders, that offenders will be convicted by the courts, and that convicted offenders will be punished;[11] this hypothesis

11 From an economic point of view, a victim would report a crime if the expected gains from reporting exceeded the expected costs. The gains and losses would include both monetary and psychic variables. In the case of property crimes a victim cannot collect insurance unless the crime is reported. This gain is independent of the efficiency of the police force. If, however, the expected gains of the victim include a desire to see the criminal caught and punished, this would be a direct function not only of the efficiency of the police force but also of the attitude of the courts. The expected costs of reporting a crime are the time lost in dealing with the police, which could be a function of efficiency, and the psychic costs, which might include a basic fear of police or an expectation that the experience might be degrading. In the latter case it is not clear that a more efficient police force would reduce these costs.

implies that the p, q, and S vectors should be included as variables in the Z^i vectors. A second hypothesis is that a larger proportion of actual offences will be reported in communities with larger 'victim stocks'; thus the G_C vector should be included in the Z^i vectors.

If the k_i functions in equation (2) are linear in logs, then, given these two hypotheses, equation (2) may be rewritten as

$$\ln O_i = \sum_{j=1}^{n} a_j \ln p_j + \sum_{j=1}^{n} b_j \ln q_j + \sum_{j=1}^{n} d_j \ln S_j + \sum_{j=1}^{n} g_j \ln G_{Cj}$$
$$+ \sum_{r=1}^{t} e_r \ln Y_r^i + \ln O_i^*, \qquad (i = 1, \dots n), \qquad (7)$$

where the Y_r^i are additional variables that might affect the recording process for crime i.

Substituting equation (7) into equation (6) yields

$$\ln O_i = \ln A_i + \sum_{j=1}^{n} (a_j + a_j) \ln p_j + \sum_{j=1}^{n} (\beta_j + b_j) \ln q_j$$
$$+ \sum_{j=1}^{n} (\delta_j + d_j) \ln S_j + \sum_{j=1}^{n} (\gamma_j + g_j) \ln G_{Cj}$$
$$+ \epsilon \ln G_L + \sum_{w=1}^{m} \mu_w \ln X_w^i + \sum_{r=1}^{t} e_r \ln Y_r^i,$$
$$(i = 1, \dots n). \qquad (8)$$

Unlike equation (6), equation (8) may be estimated empirically. The difficulty is that the parameter estimates of equation (8) may not allow identification of the 'true' parameter estimates of equation (6), the a, β, δ, and γ vectors.[12] The extent of the identification problem depends on the specification of

---

12 This discussion of the identification problem is based on the assumption that the mean of the distribution of individuals' probabilities of apprehension in a community is equal to the published clearance rate for that community. Suppose, however, that the mean of the distribution of individuals' probabilities is given by $p_i^* = C_i/O_i^*$, where C_i is the actual number of clearances. The supply-of-offences function then becomes

$$\ln O_i^* = \ln A + a_i \ln p_i^* + \beta_i \ln q_i + \delta_i \ln S_i,$$

where p_i^*, q_i, S_i, G_{Ci}, G_{Ci}, G_L, and X^i have been excluded in order to simplify the example. The recorded clearance rate is defined as $p_i = C_i/O_i$. Taking the natural logarithms of p_i^* and p_i, and eliminating the common variable C_i, gives

$$\ln p_i^* - \ln p_i = \ln O_i - \ln O_i^*.$$

Suppose now for simplicity that the function relating O_i to O_i^* is given by

$$\ln O_i = a_i \ln p_i + b_i \ln q_i + d_i \ln S_i + \ln O_i^*.$$

$k_i (Z_1{}^i, ..., Z_l{}^i)$. Only if a variable in equation (6) is not included in equation (7) can its associated 'true' elasticity be identified.[13] For example, if $b_1 = b_2 = ... = b_n = 0$ in equation (7), the third term on the right-hand side of equation (8) becomes

$$\sum_{j=1}^{n} \beta_j \ln q_j ,$$

and estimation will produce the vector β, the elasticity of actual offences with respect to the conviction rate vector q.

The following chapter describes the data used to measure the variables in equation (8).

With the above equations, it is possible to eliminate O_i^* and p_i^* from the aggregate supply-of-offences function and obtain

$$\ln O_i = \ln A + (a_i (1 + a_i) + a_i) \ln p_i + (b_i (1 + a_i) + \beta_i) \ln q_i$$
$$+ (d_i (1 + a_i) + \delta_i) \ln S_i.$$

Carr-Hill and Stern (1973) used the above assumption in their study of England and Wales. The use of p_i^* as the community mean is based on the assumption that all individuals (participants as well as non-participants in illegal activities) have knowledge of O_i^*, and there is no a priori reason why this should be the case.

13 It is possible that X_w^i ($w = 1, ... m$) and Y_r^i ($r = 1, ... t$) have common variables. In estimation no attempt was made to specify Y_r.

3
Data

The aggregate supply-of-offences function (8) is estimated using provincial data for eight provinces for the three years 1970 to 1972. Quebec and Alberta are excluded from the sample since the required judicial data are not available. The Yukon and Northwest Territories are excluded since data on some of the socioeconomic variables used in the model are not available for these areas.

As discussed in the previous chapter, the expected costs of illegal activities are indicated partly by the probability of apprehension, the probability of conviction, and the average sentence length to be served. The first of these variables is obtained from police data and is measured by the ratio of the number of clearances to the number of offences, referred to as the clearance rate. The numerator of the clearance rate includes all offences for which the police have sufficient evidence to lay a charge. In some cases (e.g. death of a suspect, refusal of the victim to prosecute, offences committed by juveniles) a formal charge is not made. However, since there is enough evidence for the police to lay a charge, a prospective offender could associate a cost to being a well defined suspect, even if he were not charged, so that clearances of this type have been included in the numerator.

The second measure, the probability of conviction, is obtained from judicial data and is calculated as the ratio of the number of offences resulting in convictions to the number of offences resulting in charges. This offence-based conviction rate is preferable to one based on individuals since a prospective offender who is planning several crimes will be interested not only in whether or not he will be convicted but also whether he will be convicted for all offences.[14]

Average sentence length is also derived from judicial data and is a weighted average of sentences handed down as corrected for statutory and earned remissions and parole. Appendix A contains a detailed discussion on the derivation of the sentence length variable. Sentence length data are available only for the most serious offence per person; in other words, if an individual is convicted of two or more different crimes in the same year, only the sentence received for the most serious crime is reported by Statistics Canada.[15] This could lead to some bias in the sentence length variable. As an example, consider the calculated average sentence length variable for theft. This variable is based on sentences given both to individuals convicted only of theft in the year and also to individuals convicted of both theft and a lesser charge, such as possession of stolen goods. The theft sentence for individuals who are convicted of theft along with a more serious charge, such as robbery, is excluded. The question is whether the exclusion of this latter group biases the average sentence length for theft. There will be no bias if the distribution of sentence lengths for theft for individuals convicted of theft and a more serious charge is the same as that for individuals convicted only of theft or of theft and a lesser charge. However, if courts tend to impose longer sentences on the former group our measure will underestimate the average sentence length for theft. The extent of this bias will depend on the relative importance of persons convicted of both theft and a more serious charge in the number of reported thefts (i.e. of the dependent variable); if they constitute only a small proportion of recorded thefts the bias will not be large.

Some incompatibilities exist between the police statistics, which provide data on the number of offences and clearance rates, and judicial statistics, which are used to compute conviction rates and average sentence lengths. First, the police data include seven categories that can be classified as crimes against property.

---

14 A person charged with five thefts and convicted of only one would result in an individual-based conviction rate of 100 per cent, but an offence-based conviction rate of only 20 per cent.

15 The most serious offence is selected according to the following criteria: (1) if a person was tried on several charges, the most serious offence is that for which the proceedings were carried to the furthest stage; (2) in the case of several convictions, the most serious offence is that which receives the heaviest punishment; (3) if the final proceedings on two or more charges was the same, the most serious offence is the one with the maximum penalty allowed by law; (4) if a person is prosecuted for one offence, but convicted of another, the most serious offence is the one for which the person was convicted. Cf. *Statistics of Criminal and Other Offences,* Statistics Canada, Cat. 85-201

TABLE 6

Police and judicial crime classifications

Crime	Police categories	Judicial categories
Robbery	Robbery	Robbery Robbery while armed
Breaking and entering	Breaking and entering	Breaking and entering a place Breaking and entering while armed
Theft A	Theft $50 and under Theft over $50	Theft Theft by conversion
Theft B	Theft of motor vehicle Theft $50 and under Theft over $50	Taking a motor vehicle without consent* Theft Theft by conversion
Fraud	Frauds	False pretences Fraud and corruption Forgery and uttering Impersonation at examination* Trade marks† Fraudulently obtaining food and lodging* Indecent phone calls† Fraudulently obtaining transportation† False employment record* Obtaining false billing*

NOTE: Asterisk signifies summary offence only; dagger signifies either summary or indictable offence. Convictions and sentences dealing with summary offences only are not included in the conviction rate and sentence length variables.

The judicial statistics, on the other hand, include twenty-one categories involving crimes against property with and without violence. Consequently, the judicial classifications must be aggregated to correspond as closely as possible to the police categories. The difficulty is that some criminal code offences included in the judicial crime classifications are not included in the police classifications, and vice versa. Appendix B summarizes the criminal code offences included in one set of data but not in the other; Table 6 lists the crime categories, together with the corresponding police and judicial classifications, used in this study.

Second, the basic set of judicial data dealing with charges, convictions, and length and type of sentences, deals only with indictable offences; summary offences and delinquencies are excluded.[16] The police data on the number of offences and clearances include all three groups. Only under rather strong assumptions will it be legitimate to exclude information on conviction rates and average sentence lengths for summary offences and juveniles when estimating the model. One of the following three assumptions would have to be true: first, the probability of conviction is the same for indictable offences, summary offences, and delinquencies; second, the probabilities of conviction, although not equal, are closely related; finally, a potential criminal is concerned only with the probability of conviction for indictable offences, even though he is contemplating the commission of a summary offence or a delinquency. Similar assumptions would have to apply also to the sentences associated with indictable and summary offences and delinquencies. If all of the above assumptions are invalid, then some other method of accounting for summary offences and delinquencies must be used. In the case of summary offences the assumption that the conviction rate is the same as that for indictable offences (or at least highly related) may not be unreasonable. Conviction for an offence is presumably based on evidence of guilt, and there is no reason why more or less evidence should be required in the case of a summary offence than in the case of an indictable offence. The assumption is not likely to hold in the case of the sentence length variable. Conviction of a summary offence usually results in a fine and/or imprisonment of up to six months. In an attempt to allow for differences in sentence lengths between summary and indictable offences the ratio of jail sentences to convictions for summary offences was included as an explanatory variable for those crimes that include summary offences in the dependent variable. The variable, however, proved insignificant and therefore was excluded in subsequent estimation. It should be noted that the problem associated with summary offences occurs primarily in the case of fraud. Robbery and breaking and entering are indictable offences. In the case of theft, the only summary offence is 'taking a motor vehicle without consent' (i.e. joy-riding) and is primarily a juvenile infraction.

It is highly unlikely that the conviction rate and sentence length associated with both juvenile and young male offenders are the same or even related to those of older offenders. Although young offenders over the statutory age limits

---

16 For summary offences, Statistics Canada publishes data only on the number of persons convicted and on the type of sentence (e.g. jail, fine). Without information on the number of charges and on the length of sentences it is impossible to compute conviction rates and sentence lengths as for indictable offences.

cannot, by definition, be guilty of juvenile delinquency,[17] it may be that the attitudes of these offenders towards crime, and the attitudes of the criminal justice system towards these offenders, are relatively homogeneous with those of juvenile delinquents. To test the hypothesis that young males have different criminal proclivities from the rest of the population, a variable measuring the percentage of the male population between the ages of fifteen and twenty-four is used in the estimation. The ten-to-fourteen age group was not included because of their significantly different schooling opportunities and job-market prospects. Over half of all convicted delinquents are included in the measured 'young male' variable.

The final cost associated with illegal activity is the opportunity cost of crime – the income that would have been received if time had been spent in legal activities. The returns from legal activity may be viewed by the prospective offender as having both short- and long-run components. That is, both current legitimate returns and long-run expected legitimate returns are evaluated in making the decision whether or not to engage in crime. This delineation is made because an individual (or family) whose current income falls because of a negative transitory element likely views the opportunity cost of crime differently than does a family whose permanent income is depressed.

Initially, an average real wage based on an industrial composite was used to measure the current returns available from engaging in legitimate endeavours. Predicted negative significant coefficients were not uniformly observed. One possible explanation for this perverse result is that the real wage reflects not only current returns from legal job-market prospects but also a strong victim-stock effect. If a higher real wage is associated with a larger stock of 'plunderable wealth,' higher levels of real wages would be associated with higher crime rates. Thus, real wages may be an unsatisfactory measure of short-run legitimate returns. As an alternative a current income distribution variable is used in the estimation. The variable utilized is the percentage of families earning less than one-half the median family income.[18] The predicted effect of the income distribution variable is

17 'In Prince Edward Island, Nova Scotia, New Brunswick, Ontario, Saskatchewan, Yukon and the Northwest Territories, the official age limit for a juvenile is under 16 years; in Newfoundland, under 17 years; in Quebec, Manitoba and British Columbia, under 18 years; and in Alberta, under 16 years for boys and 18 years for girls.' *Juvenile Delinquents*, 1971, Statistics Canada, Cat. 85-202, 7

18 Family income includes income from all sources. In using cross-sectional data for provinces it is difficult to know whether provincial differences in income distribution primarily measure differential responses to short-run economic forces or reflect stable, long-run structural differences between provinces. If the latter is true, differences in income distribution between provinces may in fact reflect differences in permanent income.

positive. As the proportion of families currently earning less than the 'poverty level' increases, there is a reduction in current legal economic opportunities, and hence a reduction in the opportunity cost of crime and an increase in the crime rate. Data on family income distributions are available only from the 1971 Census; hence it is necessary to assume that family income distributions (although not the median family income) are the same for the three years 1970 to 1972.

A second variable used to reflect the current opportunity cost of crime in some of the estimated equations is the unemployment rate. A positive relationship is expected between this variable and the crime rate.

To measure the long-run expected income from legitimate endeavours a measure of 'permanent' labour income is desirable. Unfortunately, none exists. However, changes in long-run labour market prospects may be reflected by changes in the labour force participation rate. For example, if labour market participants view their long-run prospects as unfavourable they may drop out of the labour market, thus reducing the participation rate. A negative relationship between the participation and crime rates is predicted.

The simultaneous inclusion of the unemployment rate, the participation rate, and income distribution in the supply-of-offences equation could make testing of the above hypotheses difficult because of possible multicollinearity between these variables. There may be a positive relation between the participation rate and the income distribution variable. An increase in families living below the poverty line attributable to transitory negative components in income could result in an increase in the participation rate through an 'added worker' effect; such a relationship is likely to be reflected more strongly in the participation rate for young males than in the total participation rate. Thus, both the total participation rate and the participation rate for young males are investigated for their influences on crime rates. The income distribution variable may also be positively related to the unemployment rate. For example, an increase in unemployment felt primarily by the less skilled and less educated may result in an increase in the proportion of families below one-half the median income, with no change in the median income. Finally, a third possibility is correlation between the participation rate and the unemployment rate. If labour force size is affected by job market opportunities, improved employment opportunities will result in a lower unemployment rate and, eventually, a higher participation rate. However, the degree of correlation is likely to be insignificant if changes in unemployment rates affect changes in the participation rates after a lag; such a lag is consistent with the view that participation rates primarily reflect long-run job market prospects.

Given the above measures of costs associated with illegal activities, it is necessary also to include a measure of gains from those activities. There are, of course, no published data on the expected gains from different property crimes (i.e. $G_{C1}, \ldots G_{Cn}$). An attempt has been made to allow for the influence of these variables by including a measure of the victim stock of the community, the assumption being that illegal gains expected from individual property crimes are proportional to the size of the victim stock. Statistics Canada publishes annual estimates of the number of households having televisions, record players, automobiles, radios, and so forth. The data do not permit an accurate valuation and aggregation of the total victim stock, but the elements in the matrix of correlation coefficients for the number of households with the various categories of durables in all cases display values larger than 0.9. Thus, as any single component of the victim stock increases the total number of physical units of durables included in the victim stock likely increases in substantially the same manner. The variable 'number of households with record-playing equipment' was utilized in the estimation on the basis of having the highest average correlation coefficient with all other categories of durables listed by Statistics Canada.

Other variables are also included in the supply-of-offences equation in order to test specific hypotheses and to allow for structural differences between the provinces that could significantly affect provincial crime rates. This permits more efficient estimates of the parameters associated with the crime control variables.

First, the proportion of the population that was North American Indian in 1971 is included as an explanatory variable. The distribution is assumed to be the same for the three years 1970 to 1972. This variable is included to allow for the possibility that North American Indians face an opportunity cost of crime lower than that faced by non-Indians. In other words, the hypothesis is that Indians experience poorer job market opportunities (perhaps because of discrimination) than non-Indians, which in turn is reflected in a relatively higher propensity to engage in crime.

Second, as mentioned above, the proportion of males between fifteen and twenty-four years of age is included as an explanatory variable. Several hypotheses, in addition to the reasons given earlier, suggest inclusion of this variable. As with Indians, young people may have a relatively low opportunity cost of crime compared to other age groups. Moreover, young males may derive substantially different psychic benefits from crime than other groups in the population. A related hypothesis is that young males have relatively less respect for the law and for the agencies of the criminal justice system. If these hypotheses are correct an increase in the proportion of the male population that is young should increase the crime rate, that is, the predicted sign of the coefficient of this variable is positive. For certain crimes, however, these effects may be overshadowed by the younger group's having fewer illegitimate opportunities and/or not having acquired the human capital to commit certain crimes successfully. For example, fraud (especially embezzlement) requires a certain sophistication and opportunities not generally available to the young. Robbery is a crime that is usually committed fairly late in a criminal career, presumably because the psychic costs of committing a crime which carries a threat of violence is lower for a person who has been involved in the criminal milieu for a considerable length of time. If these hypotheses are correct, if older people do have higher crime rates for robbery and fraud than younger people, the sign of the coefficient of the young male variable will be negative, that is, as the proportion of young males increases (older males decrease), the aggregate crime rate for robbery and fraud will fall.

The symbols of the variables discussed above are listed below:

P clearance rate; number of clearances divided by number of offences

Q conviction rate; number of convictions divided by number of charges

S weighted average of sentences handed down corrected for remissions and parole (see appendix A)

VS   number of households with record players (a component of the victim stock)

DIST   percentage of families with income less than one-half the median family income

UN   total unemployment rate

PR   total participation rate

$UN_{14\text{-}24}$ unemployment rate for males fourteen to twenty-four years of age

$PR_{14\text{-}24}$ participation rate for males fourteen to twenty-four years of age

$A_{15\text{-}24}$ percentage of males fifteen to twenty-four years of age in the total male population

IND   percentage of North American Indians in the population.

4
Empirical results

This chapter summarizes the two-stage least squares estimates of the aggregate supply-of-offences equation for the four property crime categories, robbery, theft A, theft B, break and enter, and fraud.[19] The following assumptions are imposed in estimating the offence equations.

1 The cross elasticities with respect to P, Q, and S in the case of the offence equation, and P and Q in the case of the police production functions and the expenditure function are constrained to be zero. This assumption is necessary because of the small sample size.

2 The first stage regression included the following exogenous and predetermined variables:

$$\ln P_i = a_0 + a_{1,i} \ln Q_i + a_{2,i} \ln S_i + a_{3,i} \ln VS + a_{4,i} \ln DIST$$

$$+ a_{5,i} \ln O_{t-1} + a_{6,i} \ln O_{PER} + a_{7,i} \ln O_{PER_{t-1}}$$

$$+ a_{8,i} \ln MVR_t + a_{9,i} \ln MVR_{t-1} + a_{10,i} \ln POP_{t-1}$$

$$+ a_{11,i} \ln E_{t-1} + a_{12,i} \ln DEN. \quad (9)$$

19 Little is known about the small sample properties of two-stage least squares. Two-stage least squares estimation has the asymptotic property of consistency, and the t-values are asymptotically normal. For the purpose of judging significance a 5 per cent significance level with critical values of 1.645 for a one-tailed test and 1.960 for a two-tailed test was used.

This equation was expanded to include the Indian, age, and labour force variables when the latter were included in the offence equation.

The variable MVR is the number of motor vehicle registrations per capita and is used in place of the traffic offence rate O_{TRAF} in the police production function. The possibility that the reported clearance rate could be influenced by the population density was allowed for by including the variable DEN, which measures the percentage of the population living in census agglomeration areas of 25,000 or more and in census metropolitan areas in 1971. The distribution for each province in 1971 was assumed to be the same in 1970 and 1972.

The lagged values of O (aggregate property crime rate), O_{PER}, MVR, and E are included in the reduced form equation as a result of two assumptions: first, that police budgets are made at the beginning of the year and hence are based on the previous year's crime rates; and second, that current expenditures on police do not adjust immediately to long-run desired expenditures. Finally, the population of the province POP is used as a proxy for the tax base in the expenditure function, and hence its lagged value is included in the reduced form equation.

Two-stage least squares estimates of the offence equation are also obtained by assuming both the clearance rate and sentence length endogenous. This second estimation is justified if, for example, courts respond to higher reported offence rates by imposing longer sentences on convicted criminals. The results are reported in appendix C. The conviction rate is always taken as exogenous on the assumption that the determination of guilt or innocence is independent of changes in the crime rate, the clearance rates and sentence lengths. It may be, however, that clearance and conviction rates are related through the amount of evidence implicitly required by police to lay a charge. For example, consider two police jurisdictions which differ in this respect. The jurisdiction which requires stronger evidence will likely have a higher conviction rate, ceteris paribus, since fewer charges would be laid, but each charge would be supported by relatively strong evidence. This relationship may be particularly strong when comparing rural and urban police forces. In rural areas the local police officers may have developed, through experience, sufficient knowledge of local judges to accurately predict whether a given amount of evidence will result in a conviction. Thus, charges are more likely to result in convictions if the officer only makes arrests when he feels he can obtain a conviction.[20] In urban areas, police officers

---

20 The relationship will be less strong if a jury, rather than a judge, adjudicates. However, Canada relies heavily upon adjudication by judges without jury. For example, of 793 total offenders sentenced for unarmed robbery in 1971, only 64 were tried by judge and jury (*Statistics of Criminal and Other Offences, 1971*, Statistics Canada, Cat. 85-201, 166). For further discussion of the relative power of judges in Canada, see Hogarth, 1967.

TABLE 7

Regression estimates of the offence equations: two-stage least squares, clearance rate endogenous

Intercept	ln $\hat{P}$	ln Q	ln S	ln DIST	ln VS	R^2
Theft A						
−3.124	−0.737	−1.842	0.035	1.331	0.186	0.980
(−10.731)	(−4.677)	(−4.197)	(0.951)	(12.272)	(12.187)	
Theft B						
−3.242	−0.786	−1.565	0.076	1.412	0.181	0.981
(−11.014)	(−4.793)	(−3.503)	(2.332)	(14.618)	(12.397)	
Fraud						
−10.953	−0.706	−0.587	−0.009	3.356	0.319	0.949
(−10.011)	(−1.576)	(−0.476)	(−0.806)	(10.373)	(7.467)	
Break and enter						
−4.962	−1.521	0.670	0.235	1.478	0.090	0.921
(−4.811)	(−4.863)	(0.646)	(1.554)	(6.265)	(2.624)	
Robbery						
−8.131	−0.833	−2.834	0.497	0.871	0.280	0.913
(−5.284)	(−2.760)	(−5.428)	(4.333)	(1.933)	(4.524)	

NOTE: Numbers in parentheses are t-values.

have less information because of the complicated court structure. Thus, other things equal, rural areas might be expected to have lower clearance rates but higher conviction rates. No attempt was made to test this hypothesis in the current study; it remains an interesting question for future research.

3 The following stochastic assumptions on the variance-covariance matrix of the offence equations are made. First, homoscedasticity is assumed. For both the ordinary and the two-stage least squares estimates a test for heteroscedastic errors suggested by Goldfeld and Quandt (1965) was made. In nearly all the equations there was not sufficient evidence to reject the assumption of homoscedastic errors. For this reason unweighted two-stage least squares estimation is used. Second, it is assumed that there is zero covariance between error terms for different crimes.

4 Finally, it is assumed that the structure of the model was stable over the three-year period.

Despite weaknesses in the data the results from the estimation do provide some tentative support for the basic hypotheses of the economic model of crime. The major findings, based on Tables 7 through 10, are now summarized and interpreted.

TABLE 8

Regression estimates of the offence equations including Indian and age variables: two-stage least squares, clearance rate endogenous

Intercept	ln $\hat{P}$	ln Q	ln S	ln DIST	ln VS	ln IND	ln $A_{15\text{-}24}$	R^2
Theft A								
-2.549 (-5.560)	-0.675 (-4.352)	-1.888 (-4.515)	-0.004 (-0.009)	1.187 (8.626)	0.169 (9.405)	0.036 (1.575)		0.983
-2.762 (-4.494)	-0.828 (-3.922)	-1.860 (-4.081)	0.041 (1.063)	1.368 (10.908)	0.193 (10.098)		0.381 (0.671)	0.979
-2.502 (-4.077)	-0.693 (-3.102)	-1.890 (-4.368)	-0.001 (-0.024)	1.199 (6.932)	0.171 (6.996)	0.034 (1.351)	0.070 (0.120)	0.983
Theft B								
-2.728 (-6.090)	-0.762 (-4.799)	-1.590 (-3.690)	0.037 (0.902)	1.274 (9.526)	0.165 (9.339)	0.032 (1.479)		0.983
-3.008 (-5.441)	-0.854 (-3.929)	-1.550 (-3.332)	0.083 (2.266)	1.450 (11.894)	0.187 (10.110)		0.272 (0.508)	0.980
-2.666 (-4.522)	-0.786 (-3.650)	-1.584 (-3.537)	0.041 (0.853)	1.290 (7.691)	0.168 (7.392)	0.031 (1.338)	0.092 (0.172)	0.983
Fraud								
-10.391 (-6.441)	-0.562 (-1.026)	-0.314 (-0.227)	-0.009 (-0.841)	3.195 (6.819)	0.319 (7.266)	0.026 (0.486)		0.949
-13.534 (-10.539)	-0.713 (-1.890)	-0.266 (-0.254)	0.001 (0.089)	3.139 (11.104)	0.256 (6.089)		-2.135 (-2.888)	0.966
-15.374 (-7.353)	-1.030 (-2.189)	-0.787 (-0.693)	0.005 (0.456)	3.439 (8.837)	0.242 (5.532)	-0.059 (-1.109)	-2.641 (-3.060)	0.968

TABLE 8 continued

Intercept	$\ln \hat{P}$	$\ln Q$	$\ln S$	$\ln$ DIST	$\ln$ VS	$\ln$ IND	$\ln A_{15\text{-}24}$	R^2
Break and enter								
-4.340 (-2.381)	-1.354 (-2.646)	0.394 (0.321)	0.207 (1.248)	1.342 (3.324)	0.089 (2.641)	0.021 (0.412)		0.927
-4.263 (-3.294)	-1.690 (-4.575)	0.610 (0.565)	0.240 (1.523)	1.613 (5.709)	0.095 (2.638)		0.806 (0.964)	0.920
-4.071 (-2.076)	-1.624 (-2.599)	0.515 (0.393)	0.229 (1.290)	1.560 (3.147)	0.095 (2.592)	0.0074 (0.132)	0.774 (0.878)	0.922
Robbery								
-5.298 (-4.175)	-0.863 (-4.034)	-1.840 (4.235)	0.374 (4.348)	0.187 (0.526)	0.219 (4.774)	0.282 (4.361)		0.959
-12.357 (-6.189)	-0.554 (-2.017)	-2.775 (-6.261)	0.276 (2.207)	0.147 (0.318)	0.172 (2.656)		-4.646 (-2.796)	0.941
-8.686 (-5.311)	-0.662 (-3.417)	-1.940 (-5.308)	0.236 (2.676)	-0.227 (-0.679)	0.152 (3.333)	0.242 (4.311)	-3.281 (-2.724)	0.973

NOTE: Numbers in parentheses are t-values.

TABLE 9

Regression estimates of the offence equations including Indian, age, and labour force activity variables: two-stage least squares, clearance rate endogenous

Intercept	$\ln \hat{P}$	$\ln Q$	$\ln S$	$\ln$ DIST	$\ln$ VS	$\ln$ UN	$\ln$ PR	$\ln$ IND	$\ln A_{15\text{-}24}$	R^2
Theft A										
-0.553 (-0.413)	-0.867 (-5.944)	-1.518 (-3.635)	0.189 (3.133)	1.608 (12.119)	0.259 (9.264)	0.102 (1.828)	-1.022 (-2.397)			0.986
-1.084 (-0.924)	-0.756 (-5.625)	-1.433 (-3.975)	0.127 (2.167)	1.388 (9.239)	0.230 (8.445)	0.153 (2.892)	-0.677 (-1.707)	0.047 (2.242)		0.991
-0.554 (-0.399)	-0.866 (-4.701)	-1.518 (-3.505)	0.189 (3.023)	1.608 (11.573)	0.259 (8.938)	0.102 (1.766)	-1.022 (-2.238)		-0.004 (-0.007)	0.986
-1.316 (-1.154)	-0.636 (-3.717)	-1.379 (-3.967)	0.120 (2.123)	1.322 (8.467)	0.222 (8.180)	0.168 (3.203)	-0.721 (-1.894)	0.057 (2.579)	-0.470 (-1.062)	0.992
Theft B										
-1.019 (-0.726)	-0.855 (-5.202)	-1.322 (-3.055)	0.210 (3.435)	1.667 (12.540)	0.243 (8.583)	0.077 (1.383)	-0.870 (-1.922)			0.986
-1.608 (-1.254)	-0.753 (-4.881)	-1.253 (-3.238)	0.146 (2.337)	1.439 (8.994)	0.215 (7.518)	0.134 (2.367)	-0.512 (-1.171)	0.057 (2.117)		0.989
-1.104 (-0.759)	-0.817 (-4.080)	-1.316 (-2.977)	0.211 (3.365)	1.653 (11.721)	0.242 (8.313)	0.081 (1.396)	-0.899 (-1.915)		-0.174 (-0.354)	0.986
-1.992 (-1.557)	-0.612 (-3.249)	-1.222 (-3.255)	0.133 (2.174)	1.351 (7.910)	0.206 (7.169)	0.158 (2.717)	-0.530 (-1.250)	0.055 (2.477)	-0.545 (-1.235)	0.991

TABLE 9 continued

Intercept	ln $\hat{P}$	ln Q	ln S	ln DIST	ln VS	ln UN	ln PR	ln IND	ln A_{15-24}	R^2
Fraud										
-13.272 (-4.062)	-0.695 (-1.496)	-0.247 (-0.176)	-0.009 (-0.746)	3.329 (9.844)	0.315 (6.422)	0.116 (0.778)	0.563 (0.750)			0.951
-9.239 (-2.090)	-0.052 (-0.079)	0.638 (0.406)	-0.021 (-1.426)	2.607 (4.202)	0.356 (6.111)	0.332 (1.528)	0.023 (0.027)	0.149 (1.406)		0.951
-11.369 (-4.587)	-0.658 (-1.906)	-1.155 (-1.081)	-0.002 (-0.188)	3.086 (11.907)	0.267 (6.920)	0.089 (0.798)	-1.126 (-1.572)		-3.458 (-3.762)	0.975
-9.290 (-2.758)	-0.307 (-0.602)	-0.604 (-0.479)	-0.009 (-0.759)	2.707 (5.713)	0.293 (6.035)	0.209 (1.231)	-1.301 (-1.674)	0.082 (0.981)	-3.210 (-3.199)	0.974
Break and enter										
-7.574 (-2.964)	-1.636 (-5.380)	1.267 (1.183)	0.319 (2.021)	1.593 (6.668)	0.096 (2.656)	0.173 (1.658)	0.434 (0.723)			0.929
-5.092 (-2.724)	-0.815 (-2.330)	0.050 (0.061)	0.233 (2.187)	0.917 (3.233)	0.111 (4.635)	0.371 (3.822)	0.455 (1.174)	0.134 (2.836)		0.972
-7.533 (-2.839)	-1.761 (-5.217)	1.250 (1.124)	0.321 (1.954)	1.714 (6.263)	0.097 (2.578)	0.166 (1.529)	0.710 (1.050)		0.984 (1.047)	0.928
-4.764 (-2.408)	-0.661 (-1.312)	-0.112 (-0.127)	0.221 (2.053)	0.784 (1.855)	0.113 (4.770)	0.400 (3.391)	0.366 (0.845)	0.152 (2.389)	-0.328 (-0.415)	0.976

TABLE 9 continued

Intercept	ln $\hat{P}$	ln Q	ln S	ln DIST	ln VS	ln UN	ln PR	ln IND	ln A_{15-24}	R^2
Robbery										
−11.258	−0.962	−2.433	0.380	0.584	0.177	−0.409	1.396			0.943
(−1.956)	(−3.931)	(−5.069)	(2.626)	(1.345)	(2.353)	(−1.690)	(0.859)			
−9.533	−0.872	−1.800	0.304	0.109	0.176	−0.019	1.238	0.243		0.962
(−1.948)	(−4.173)	(−3.829)	(2.423)	(0.267)	(2.779)	(−0.075)	(0.903)	(2.640)		
−11.174	−0.806	−2.534	0.321	0.292	0.154	−0.351	0.488		−2.794	0.952
(−2.053)	(−3.166)	(−5.518)	(2.246)	(0.639)	(2.120)	(−1.509)	(0.294)		(−1.471)	
−9.310	−0.683	−1.872	0.229	−0.268	0.149	0.078	0.164	0.260	−3.269	0.973
(−2.194)	(−3.413)	(−4.580)	(2.009)	(−0.682)	(2.660)	(0.349)	(0.128)	(3.249)	(−2.216)	

NOTE: Numbers in parenthesis are t-values.

TABLE 10

Regression estimates of the offence equations, including Indian, age and labour activity (males aged fourteen to twenty-four) variables: two-stage least squares, clearance rate endogenous

Intercept	ln $\hat{P}$	ln Q	ln S	ln DIST	ln VS	ln UN$_{14-24}$	ln PR$_{14-24}$	ln IND	ln A_{15-24}	R^2
Theft A										
-3.932	-0.780	-1.441	0.091	1.444	0.211	0.122	0.007			0.983
(-3.028)	(-4.451)	(-2.888)	(1.906)	(10.087)	(10.611)	(1.619)	(0.020)			
-3.004	-0.725	-1.333	0.059	1.276	0.195	0.180	-0.101	0.063		0.990
(-2.813)	(-5.199)	(-3.366)	(1.509)	(10.221)	(11.871)	(2.891)	(-0.356)	(3.156)		
-3.807	-0.835	-1.446	0.093	1.459	0.216	0.124	0.060		0.295	0.983
(-2.778)	(-3.962)	(-2.787)	(1.871)	(9.626)	(9.482)	(1.585)	(0.156)		(0.520)	
-3.044	-0.608	-1.302	0.048	1.212	0.182	0.188	-0.225	0.076	-0.564	0.992
(-2.983)	(-3.645)	(-3.434)	(1.246)	(9.210)	(9.516)	(3.143)	(-0.774)	(3.433)	(-1.170)	
Theft B										
-4.298	-0.763	-1.215	0.121	1.491	0.203	0.114	0.125			0.984
(-3.352)	(-4.089)	(-2.476)	(2.624)	(10.670)	(10.401)	(1.517)	(0.352)			
-3.328	-0.784	-1.097	0.091	1.343	0.188	0.163	-0.023	0.056		0.989
(-2.917)	(-4.871)	(-2.629)	(2.251)	(10.340)	(10.898)	(2.470)	(-0.075)	(2.729)		
-4.216	-0.797	-1.210	0.123	1.502	0.205	0.113	0.152		0.168	0.983
(-3.102)	(-3.557)	(-2.372)	(2.544)	(10.025)	(9.406)	(1.446)	(0.400)		(0.306)	
-3.393	-0.677	-1.091	0.082	1.289	0.179	0.173	-0.117	0.065	-0.447	0.990
(-3.051)	(-3.718)	(-2.687)	(2.018)	(9.268)	(9.268)	(2.660)	(-0.374)	(2.928)	(-0.927)	

TABLE 10 continued

Intercept	ln $\hat{P}$	ln Q	ln S	ln DIST	ln VS	ln UN$_{14\text{-}24}$	ln PR$_{14\text{-}24}$	ln IND	ln A$_{15\text{-}24}$	R^2
Fraud										
-16.993	-0.652	0.724	-0.004	3.078	0.340	0.291	1.507			0.962
(-6.265)	(-1.729)	(0.567)	(-0.395)	(9.587)	(8.269)	(1.962)	(2.324)			
-15.734	-0.495	0.892	-0.009	2.934	0.347	0.345	1.280	0.045		0.962
(-3.711)	(-0.891)	(0.642)	(-0.550)	(5.964)	(7.590)	(1.681)	(1.451)	(0.397)		
-15.710	-0.767	-0.251	-0.002	3.182	0.269	0.219	0.206		-2.469	0.972
(-6.407)	(-2.285)	(-0.209)	(-0.253)	(11.114)	(5.689)	(1.632)	(0.258)		(-2.327)	
-13.699	-0.525	-0.021	-0.010	2.960	0.277	0.301	-0.195	0.071	-2.555	0.972
(-3.575)	(-1.076)	(-0.017)	(-0.684)	(6.847)	(5.523)	(1.661)	(-0.194)	(0.764)	(-2.314)	
Break and enter										
-9.361	-1.537	1.550	0.351	1.507	0.120	0.260	0.837			0.940
(-3.591)	(-4.811)	(1.516)	(2.366)	(5.910)	(3.307)	(2.201)	(1.327)			
-6.669	-0.889	0.332	0.250	0.997	0.124	0.385	0.663	0.110		0.971
(-3.040)	(-2.488)	(0.370)	(2.170)	(3.521)	(4.739)	(3.847)	(1.442)	(2.362)		
-9.356	-1.638	1.585	0.363	1.586	0.134	0.267	1.175		1.105	0.942
(-3.537)	(-4.914)	(1.528)	(2.407)	(5.968)	(3.492)	(2.230)	(1.702)		(1.305)	
-6.754	-0.915	0.373	0.253	1.018	0.125	0.381	0.686	0.107	0.059	0.970
(-2.519)	(-1.618)	(0.324)	(1.867)	(2.280)	(4.285)	(3.186)	(1.113)	(1.419)	(0.061)	

TABLE 10 continued

Intercept	ln $\hat{P}$	ln Q	ln S	ln DIST	ln VS	ln UN_{14-24}	ln PR_{14-24}	ln IND	ln A_{15-24}	R^2
Robbery										
-18.930	-0.847	-2.077	0.170	-0.316	0.217	-0.002	3.852			0.960
(-3.856)	(-3.715)	(-4.930)	(1.287)	(-0.679)	(4.516)	(-0.009)	(2.818)			
-15.171	-0.791	-1.711	0.181	-0.376	0.214	0.187	2.877	0.188		0.970
(-3.196)	(-3.832)	(-4.121)	(1.520)	(-0.896)	(4.955)	(0.769)	(2.196)	(2.141)		
-18.720	-0.764	-2.164	0.151	-0.362	0.196	0.003	3.337		-1.332	0.962
(-3.781)	(-2.978)	(-4.910)	(1.113)	(-0.766)	(3.425)	(0.011)	(2.155)		(-0.726)	
-13.616	-0.593	-1.794	0.142	-0.494	0.166	0.253	1.465	0.242	-2.917	0.976
(-3.028)	(-2.679)	(-4.615)	(1.259)	(-1.252)	(3.411)	(1.106)	(1.010)	(2.786)	(-1.795)	

NOTE: Numbers in parentheses are t-values.

A significant inverse relationship is generally found between the reported crime rate and the clearance rate (probability of apprehension) for the two theft classifications, break and enter, and robbery. The estimated elasticities for the probability of apprehension are always less than one in absolute value for both theft classifications and robbery, with very little difference in the range of estimates. For break and enter, the elasticity estimates are generally greater than one in absolute value. The clearance rate for fraud becomes significant in a number of equations when the proportion of the male population between the ages of fifteen and twenty-four is included.

The conviction rate is negative and significantly related to the recorded crime rate for robbery and the two theft classifications, with the estimated elasticities always greater than one in absolute value. There is no evidence that conviction rates influence recorded crime rates for fraud and break and enter.

For the equations reported in Tables 7 to 10, the predicted inverse relationship between expected sentence lengths and crime rates does not appear. In fact, for some of the robbery, theft, and break-and-enter equations a significant positive relationship is found.

The elasticity estimates for the income distribution variable are generally positive, significant, and greater than one for theft, fraud, and break and enter. For these crimes the t-values are not significantly affected by the inclusion of the young male and labour force variables, but are affected by the inclusion of the North American Indian variable. Inclusion of the latter variable results in a decline in the t-values for income distribution in a number of equations, possibly indicating some collinearity between the family income distribution variable and the percentage of the population North American Indian.

The victim stock measure is positive and significant for all crimes and all equations as predicted. The elasticities are generally less than unity.[21]

The young male variable A_{15-24} is significant only for the crime categories found and robbery. For these crimes the larger the proportion of the male population aged fifteen to twenty-four, the lower are the fraud and robbery crime rates.

---

21 The elasticities for the victim stock measure the relative response of offences to changes in record playing equipment, a component of the victim stock. Hence, the estimates overstate the elasticities for the total victim stock. To see this, assume that the victim stock VS is composed of three components, X, Y, Z, where VS $= X + Y + Z$, $Y = aX$, $a > 0$, and $Z = bX$ $b > 0$. The offence function then becomes

$$O = \beta VS + \ldots$$
$$= \beta (X + Y + Z) + \ldots$$
$$= \beta (1 + a + b)X + \ldots$$

where β is the elasticity of the victim stock and $\beta (1 + a + b)$ is the estimated elasticity. Since $a > 0$ and $b > 0$, the estimate is larger than β, but β remains positive.

The significance of the variable representing the proportion of the population that is North American Indian depends largely upon whether labour force variables are also included in the equation. If so, the North American Indian coefficient is generally significant, positive, and less than one in value for robbery, break and enter, and the theft classifications. The interpretation of this result must be made with some care. Indians living on reserves are not included in the labour force statistics, so that the labour force experience of these Indians is not being measured by the labour force variables included in the equations. Rather, labour market discrimination against Indians on reserves would be registered in the coefficient of the North American Indian variable.

The labour force variables are rather weak and mixed. For the total (i.e. all ages and both sexes) labour force the unemployment rate is found to be significant and positive (as predicted) for some of the theft and break and enter equations. The participation rate is negative and significant (as predicted) only for some of the theft equations. Concerning the labour force experience of young males the unemployment rate is again positive and significant for some of the theft and break and enter equations, whereas the participation rate is generally significant only for robbery, but with a (perverse) positive coefficient.

A few interpretative comments with respect to the empirical results are in order.

The results indicate the importance of the two risk variables in affecting crimes rates. The relative strength of the conviction rate is surprising. At least for robbery and theft, prospective offenders respond to courtroom proceedings more than is generally thought. This is understandable for crimes typically committed only after substantial criminal experience has been obtained — relatively low costs are associated with being charged since the offender is already known to police through his criminal record. The insignificance of the conviction rate for fraud might be explained by the possibility of these offenders losing their jobs if charged, regardless of whether a conviction is obtained. Thus a relatively large cost is associated with the clearance rate. The insignificance of the conviction rate for break and enter is at least partially explained by the large number of such offences that are cleared by convictions for possessing stolen goods. The assumption of zero cross-elasticities between these two crimes may be unwarranted. A supply-of-offences function for possessing stolen goods was originally included in the estimation, but the results were poor. It is likely that such a function does not exist; offenders rarely set out to commit a 'possessing stolen goods' offence, but rather, in accordance with rules of evidence, are charged with this when committing a more serious crime.

The insignificant and positive significant relationships between sentence lengths and offence rates is puzzling. As indicated in the introduction, the technique used here for deriving expected sentence lengths militates against picking up effects other than deterrent effects, relative to techniques used by other researchers.[22] However, as noted in the discussion on identification, these results do not preclude the possibility of an inverse relationship between the true offence rate and expected sentence length. A further consideration is that the model may be misspecified in the following sense: judges may decree more severe sentences in response to observed increases in the crime rate. This would explain the positive relationships found in Tables 7 to 10. If such a simultaneous relationship holds, the proper econometric procedure is to treat both the clearance rate and sentence length as determined within the model. Appendix C presents two-stage least squares estimates of the supply-of-offences equations under these assumptions. As discussed in that appendix, there is some evidence that judges do respond to increases in crime rates for certain crimes with longer sentences. One final explanation for insignificant sentence lengths is that prospective offenders heavily discount the future. That is to say, one difference between offenders and non-offenders may be that the former have higher rates of time preference.[23] This hypothesis suggests not only insignificant sentence lengths but also weak responses to changes in long-run expected income. In fact, poor results were obtained for the participation rate, which was used as a proxy for 'long-run legitimate labour market income.'

As previously noted, a difficulty with using the participation rate as an indicator of changes in long-run legitimate labour market prospects is that the participation rate may also be reflecting a short-run 'added worker' effect. It was hypothesized that this effect would more likely materialize when examining marginal groups in the labour force, including young males. Thus, as current

22 Under certain conditions the positive relationship between sentence length and crime rates could be attributed to 'negative training' while incarcerated. For example, consider two areas, A and B, identical except $S_A > S_B$ in all periods. Let $O_A{}^D$ and $O_B{}^D$ represent crime rates in the areas if there were only a deterrent effect, and $O_A{}^T$ and $O_B{}^T$ represent crime rates attributable to 'negative training.' Then, since $S_A > S_B$, $O_A{}^D < O_B{}^D$ and $O_A{}^T > O_B{}^T$. If $O_A{}^D + O_A{}^T > O_B{}^D + O_B{}^T$, a positive correlation would result between sentence length and current aggregate crime rates. However, suppose $S_A < S_B$ in the current period only; then $O_A{}^D > O_B{}^D$ but $O_A{}^T > O_B{}^T$ since $S_A > S_B$ in past periods. In this case $O_A{}^D + O_A{}^T > O_B{}^D + O_B{}^T$, resulting in a negative correlation between current offence rates and sentence length. Thus, even though there exists a negative deterrent effect in both cases, the observed aggregate relationship can vary. As noted in the introduction the measure of expected sentence length used in the study is not based on sentence lengths served by current period releasees and hence is less likely to reflect past period sentences.

23 The authors are indebted to Gerald Walter of the University of Victoria for this observation.

income prospects decline and more crime is committed a simultaneous increase may be seen in the participation rate of young males. In comparing the empirical results of Tables 9 and 10, it appears that this hypothesis is correct. For every crime and every equation the coefficient of the participation rate for young males is larger than for the total participation rate. The participation rate for young males therefore cannot be taken to reflect long-run legitimate labour market prospects.

Although the results generally support the economic model of crime, considerable differences are found in the supply-of-offences functions between different crime categories. Fraud and robbery are not a young man's crimes, as indicated by the negative significant elasticities for the age variable. This result is consistent with the hypothesis that considerable criminal experience is needed to be successful in fraud and that the psychic costs of committing a crime threatening violence (robbery) are reduced by longer exposure to criminal activity. The variables representing the current opportunity cost of crime – income distribution and the unemployment rate – are insignificant for robbery in all but one equation (Table 7); the interpretation is that the prospective robber does not see the legitimate labour market as a viable alternative to criminal activity, and this result is again consistent with the view that robbery is a crime associated with the later stages of the criminal career. The strength of the elasticity of the income distribution variable for fraud vis-à-vis other crimes is consistent with the view of fraud as a white-collar crime induced by a relative reduction in standards of living; as white-collar families are pushed below what they consider to be an income level sufficient to maintain their social status an attempt is made to re-establish that status by obtaining income from fraudulent activities.

5
Range of elasticities for 'true' offence rates: an illustration

In the second chapter it was observed that if the recorded offence rate differs from the actual offence rate, then the estimated elasticities may not accurately reflect the response of *actual* crime rates to changes in explanatory variables. The extent of the identification problem depends upon the recording function; the elasticity for any variable included in the supply-of-offences function but excluded from the recording function can be identified directly. To identify the 'actual' offence elasticities of variables included in the recording function, knowledge of the recording function is required.

For illustrative purposes this chapter presents a range of estimates of the true elasticities under the assumption that the recording rate is a function of the clearance rate and sentence length only. In this situation the recording function for each crime can be written as

$$K = P^a S^d, \tag{10}$$

where the subscripts identifying crime types have been deleted for simplification. Both parameters are assumed to be positive. The higher the clearance rate, the greater is the willingness of the public to report crimes, because in this case the public has a higher expectation that the offender will be apprehended. Similarly, if victims have a strong desire to see offenders punished (a vengeance motive) then the more severe the punishment the greater is the willingness of victims to report crimes.

From the estimated offence equations the elasticities associated with P and S represent a combined deterrent and recording effect; that is,

$$(a + a) = \hat{\theta}_1, \quad a > 0, \tag{11}$$

$$(\delta + d) = \hat{\theta}_2, \quad d > 0, \tag{12}$$

where a and δ are the elasticities of the true offence rate with respect to the probability of apprehension and the expected sentence length respectively. Equations (10), (11), and (12) are three equations in five unknowns (K, a, d, a, δ). Although it is impossible to identify a and δ, a range of estimates for these 'true' elasticities can be derived for different assumed values of a, d, and K.

To accomplish the identification, equation (10) is first solved for the parameter a: :

$$\frac{\ln K - d \ln S}{\ln P} = a > 0. \tag{13}$$

The mean values for the data samples of S and P are inserted in equation (13). For a given value of the recording rate K and an assumed value for d, it is possible to derive an estimate of a. This estimate may then be subtracted from $\hat{\theta}_1$ to obtain an estimate of a. The fact that both a and d are assumed positive, and K and P are between 0 and 1, implies certain constraints on the parameters of the recording function. With K and P less than 1 the associated natural logs are negative. In order for the parameter a to be positive this implies (from equation 13) that[24]

$$\frac{\ln K}{\ln \bar{S}} < d. \tag{14}$$

Inequality (14) holds only if the mean sentence length is greater than one month, since $\ln \bar{S} > 0$ only if $\bar{S} > 1$. This is the case for fraud, break and enter, and robbery. For these crimes, inequality (14) implies that d must be greater than some negative number. Since we are constraining d to be a positive number, this implies that d can assume any positive value. One might hazard a guess that a 1 per cent increase in sentence length results in less than a 1 per cent increase in the recording ratio, which implies that $0 < d < 1$. However, for the sake of completeness, d is assigned values between 0.5 and 2.5 in the following tables.

---

24 Since $\ln P < 0$, in order for $a > 0$, $\ln K - d \ln S < 0$, this condition is equivalent to $\ln K / \ln S < d$ if $\ln S > 0$.

TABLE 11

Estimated elasticities for the actual offence rate in theft, with respect to P and S, for different reporting rates

		Theft A					Theft B			
		$\hat{\theta}$ for P		$\hat{\theta}$ for S			$\hat{\theta}$ for P		$\hat{\theta}$ for S	
d	a	−0.596	−0.867	−0.016	−0.200	a	−0.612	−0.856	0.033	0.212
K = 0.4										
0.5	0.577	−1.173	−1.444	−0.516	−0.300	0.584	−1.196	−1.440	−0.467	−0.288
1.0	0.482	−1.078	−1.349	−1.016	−0.800	0.487	−1.099	−1.343	−0.967	−0.788
1.5	0.386	−0.982	−1.253	−1.516	−1.300	0.391	−1.003	−1.247	−1.467	−1.288
1.75	0.338	−0.934	−1.235	−1.766	−1.550	0.342	−0.954	−1.198	−1.717	−1.538
1.90	0.310	−0.906	−1.177	−1.916	−1.700	0.313	−0.925	−1.169	−1.169	−1.688
K = 0.5										
0.5	0.413	−1.009	−1.280	−0.516	−0.300	0.418	−1.030	−1.274	−0.467	−0.288
1.0	0.318	−0.914	−1.185	−1.016	−0.800	0.322	−0.934	−1.178	−0.967	−0.788
1.5	0.222	−0.818	−1.089	−1.516	−1.300	0.225	−0.837	−1.081	−1.467	−1.288
1.75	0.175	−0.771	−1.042	−1.766	−1.550	0.177	−0.789	−1.033	−1.717	−1.538
1.90	0.146	−0.742	−1.013	−1.916	−1.700	0.148	−0.760	−1.004	−1.169	−1.688
K = 0.6										
0.5	0.279	−0.875	−1.146	−0.516	−0.300	0.283	−0.895	−1.139	−0.467	−0.288
1.0	0.184	−0.780	−1.051	−1.016	−0.800	0.186	−0.798	−1.042	−0.967	−0.788
1.5	0.089	−0.685	−0.956	−1.516	−1.300	0.090	−0.702	−0.946	−1.467	−1.288
1.75	0.041	−0.637	−0.908	−1.766	−1.550	0.041	−0.653	−0.897	−1.717	−1.538
1.90	0.012	−0.608	−0.879	−1.916	−1.700	0.012	−0.624	−0.868	−1.169	−1.688
K = 0.7										
0.5	0.166	−0.762	−1.033	−0.516	−0.300	0.168	−0.780	−1.024	−0.467	−0.288
1.0	0.071	−0.667	−0.938	−1.016	−0.800	0.072	−0.684	−0.928	−0.967	−0.788
K = 0.8										
0.5	0.068	−0.664	−0.935	−0.516	−0.300	0.069	−0.681	−0.925	−0.467	−0.288

NOTE: Assuming $K = P^a S^d$, certain values of K and d (and corresponding estimates) are deleted because these combinations imply a negative value of a. See text for explanation.

TABLE 12

Estimated elasticities for the actual offence rate in fraud, break and enter, and robbery, with respect to P and S, for different reporting rates

		Fraud					Break and enter					Robbery			
		$\hat{\theta}$ for P		$\hat{\theta}$ for S			$\hat{\theta}$ for P		$\hat{\theta}$ for S			$\hat{\theta}$ for P		$\hat{\theta}$ for S	
d	a	−0.052	−1.095	−0.111	0.016	a	−0.661	−1.761	0.089	0.399	a	−0.554	−1.138	0.142	1.233
K = 0.4															
0.5	2.827	−2.879	−3.922	−0.611	−0.484	1.329	−1.990	−3.090	−0.411	−0.101	2.672	−3.226	−3.810	−0.358	0.733
1.0	3.789	−3.841	−4.884	−1.111	−0.984	1.899	−2.560	−3.660	−0.911	−0.601	4.267	−4.821	−5.447	−0.858	0.233
1.5	4.750	−4.802	−5.845	−1.611	−1.484	2.469	−3.130	−4.230	−1.411	−1.101	5.862	−6.416	−7.000	−1.358	−0.267
2.0	5.711	−5.763	−6.806	−2.111	−1.984	3.039	−3.700	−4.800	−1.911	−1.601	7.457	−8.011	−8.595	−1.858	−0.767
2.5	6.672	−6.724	−7.767	−2.611	−2.484	3.609	−4.270	−5.370	−2.411	−2.101	9.052	−9.606	−10.190	−2.358	−1.267
K = 0.5															
0.5	2.373	−2.425	−3.468	−0.611	−0.484	1.144	−1.805	−2.905	−0.411	−0.101	2.410	−2.964	−3.548	−0.358	0.733
1.0	3.334	−3.386	−4.429	−1.111	−0.984	1.714	−2.375	−3.475	−0.911	−0.601	4.005	−4.559	−5.143	−0.858	0.233
1.5	4.296	−4.348	−5.391	−1.611	−1.484	2.284	−2.945	−4.045	−1.411	−1.101	5.600	−6.154	−6.738	−1.358	−0.267
2.0	5.257	−5.309	−6.352	−2.111	−1.984	2.854	−3.515	−4.615	−1.911	−1.601	7.195	−7.749	−8.333	−1.858	−0.767
2.5	6.218	−6.270	−7.313	−2.611	−2.484	3.424	−4.085	−5.185	−2.411	−2.101	8.790	−9.344	−9.928	−2.358	−1.267
K = 0.6															
0.5	2.002	−2.054	−3.097	−0.611	−0.484	0.993	−1.654	−2.754	−0.411	−0.101	2.195	−2.749	−3.333	−0.358	0.733
1.0	2.963	−3.015	−4.058	−1.111	−0.984	1.563	−2.224	−3.324	−0.911	−0.601	3.790	−4.344	−4.928	−0.858	0.733
1.5	3.924	−3.976	−5.019	−1.611	−1.484	2.133	−2.794	−3.894	−1.411	−1.101	5.385	−5.939	−6.523	−1.358	−0.267
2.0	4.885	−4.937	−5.980	−2.111	−1.984	2.703	−3.364	−4.464	−1.911	−1.601	6.980	−7.534	−8.118	−1.858	−0.767
2.5	5.846	−5.898	−6.941	−2.611	−2.484	3.273	−3.934	−5.034	−2.411	−2.101	8.575	−9.129	−9.713	−2.358	−1.267

TABLE 12 continued

		Fraud					Break and enter					Robbery			
		$\hat{\theta}$ for P		$\hat{\theta}$ for S			$\hat{\theta}$ for P		$\hat{\theta}$ for S			$\hat{\theta}$ for P		$\hat{\theta}$ for S	
d	a	−0.052	−1.095	−0.111	0.016	a	−0.661	−1.761	0.089	0.399	a	−0.554	−1.138	0.142	1.233
K = 0.7															
0.5	1.688	−1.740	−2.783	−0.611	−0.484	0.865	−1.526	−2.626	−0.411	−0.101	2.014	−2.568	−3.152	−0.358	0.733
1.0	2.649	−2.701	−3.744	−1.111	−0.984	1.435	−2.096	−3.196	−0.911	−0.601	3.609	−4.163	−4.747	−0.858	0.233
1.5	3.610	−3.662	−4.705	−1.611	−1.484	2.005	−2.666	−3.766	−1.411	−1.101	5.204	−5.758	−6.342	−1.358	−0.267
2.0	4.571	−4.623	−5.666	−2.111	−1.984	2.575	−3.236	−4.336	−1.911	−1.601	6.799	−7.353	−7.937	−1.858	−0.767
2.5	5.533	−5.585	−6.628	−2.611	−2.484	3.145	−3.806	−4.906	−2.411	−2.101	8.394	−8.948	−9.532	−2.358	−1.267
K = 0.8															
0.5	1.416	−1.468	−2.511	−0.611	−0.484	0.755	−1.416	−2.516	−0.411	−0.101	1.857	−2.411	−2.995	−0.358	0.733
1.0	2.377	−2.429	−3.472	−1.111	−0.984	1.325	−1.986	−3.086	−0.911	−0.601	3.452	−4.006	−4.588	−0.858	0.233
1.5	3.338	−3.390	−4.433	−1.611	−1.484	1.895	−2.556	−3.656	−1.411	−1.101	5.047	−5.601	−6.185	−1.358	−0.267
2.0	4.299	−4.351	−5.394	−2.111	−1.984	2.465	−3.126	−4.226	−1.911	−1.601	6.642	−7.196	−7.780	−1.858	−0.767
2.5	5.260	−5.312	−6.355	−2.611	−2.484	3.035	−3.696	−4.796	−2.411	−2.101	8.237	−8.791	−9.375	−2.358	−1.267
K = 0.9															
0.5	1.176	−1.228	−2.271	−0.611	−0.484	0.657	−1.318	−2.418	−0.411	−0.101	1.719	−2.273	−2.857	−0.358	0.733
1.0	2.137	−2.189	−3.232	−1.111	−0.984	1.227	−1.888	−2.988	−0.911	−0.601	3.314	−3.868	−4.452	−0.858	0.233
1.5	3.078	−3.130	−4.173	−1.611	−1.484	1.797	−2.458	−3.558	−1.411	−1.101	4.909	−5.463	−6.047	1.358	−0.267
2.0	4.059	−4.111	−5.154	−2.111	−1.984	2.367	−3.028	−4.128	−1.911	−1.601	6.504	−7.058	−7.642	−1.858	−0.767
2.5	5.021	−5.073	−6.116	−2.611	−2.484	2.937	−3.598	−4.698	−2.411	−2.101	8.099	−8.653	−9.237	−2.358	−1.267

NOTE: Assuming $K = P^a S^d$

For theft, $\ln \bar{S} < 0$, which implies that

$$\frac{\ln K}{\ln \bar{S}} > d. \tag{15}$$

For example, if $K = 0.6$, the ratio in (15) is approximately 2, implying that for the theft reporting function d must be a positive number between 0 and 2.[25]

Tables 11 and 12 contain elasticity estimates for true offence rates with respect to $\bar{P}$ and $\bar{S}$ for recording rates of 0.4, 0.5, 0.6, 0.7, 0.8 and 0.9. For each assumed recording rate and parameter estimate d, the associated value of a is calculated from equation (13). Estimates of a and δ are then obtained from equations (11) and (12). Values of $\hat{\theta}_1$ and $\hat{\theta}_2$ are the lowest and highest estimates derived from the two-stage least squares estimates in the previous chapter and in appendix C.

Victim studies provide information on the recording rates for different crimes. Based on a survey prepared for the President's Commission on Law Enforcement and Administration of Justice, Reynolds (1971) calculated recording rates of 0.67 for robbery, 0.33 for burglary, and 0.40 for larceny. The corresponding crime classifications in Canada for burglary and larceny are break and enter, and theft. If it can be assumed for illustrative purposes that these recording rates hold in Canada, a range of estimates of the true elasticities can be derived from Tables 11 and 12. For example, in the case of theft B the derived 'true' elasticity estimates for the clearance rate range between -0.925 and -1.440. For sentence length the 'true' elasticity estimates range from -0.288 to -1.688.

It should be stressed that the information contained in Tables 11 and 12 is purely illustrative. The information is correct only if the recording function utilized for the analysis is properly specified. For example, if increases in sentence lengths do not increase the recording ratio, then Tables 11 and 12 are erroneous: the estimated sentence length elasticity would be the true elasticity, and the true probability of apprehension elasticity would have to be recalculated using the appropriate recording function. Whether a particular variable such as sentence length is in the recording function is purely an empirical matter, and remains the subject of future research.

---

25 The value of the ratio $\ln K / \ln \bar{S}$ declines as K increases. For example, for $K = 0.9$ in Table 11, d would have to be less than 0.5 in order for a to be positive.

6
Conclusion and recommendations for future research

To summarize briefly: the economic model of property crime assumes that prospective offenders rationally weigh the expected costs and benefits of their actions in deciding whether to engage in property crime. In this study the empirical counterparts of those costs and benefits for Canadian offenders were specified in an attempt to subject the model to an empirical test. In general, the regression results presented in chapter 4 and in appendices C and D are consistent with the model.

The single pervasive result that is *not* consistent with the predictions of the model is that whereas an increased risk of capture and conviction leads to a reduction in recorded property crime rates, an increase in the severity of sentence (as measured by sentence length) does not appear to reduce the recorded crime rate. The policy implications of this result are profound. However, the findings of the study are only tentative. Before an economist (or any other social scientist, for that matter) would categorically accept such a crucial result, studies using different data sets must necessarily obtain substantially the same conclusion.[26]

26 Shortly after the current study was completed, Statistics Canada provided the authors with unpublished police and judicial data for Ontario in 1971 by census division area. Preliminary findings corroborate the results of this study. Additional hypotheses related to the deterrent effect of incarceration were tested and rejected. For example, it is often hypothesized that a reduction in the variance of sentence lengths will deter prospective offenders. The study indicates no empirical support for the hypothesis.

Therefore, one obvious suggestion is that further economic research on property crime in Canada should be undertaken. More and better Canadian data will be needed for these studies. The data base used here was a pool of time-series and cross-section observations at the provincial level. The pooling procedure was necessitated by the small number of geographical units of observation at any one point in time. The provision of unpublished police and judicial data on the basis of relatively disaggregated geographical units such as census division areas would improve the reliability of the empirical tests. Furthermore, using census areas as the units of observation permits full use of the wealth of economic and sociological variables in the census. No assumption need be made (as was necessary in this study) that these census variables remain constant over time.

In addition to simply replicating the current study using superior data, future studies should expand the use of the model. The economic model of property crime could be adapted to forecast crime rates. This would allow policy-makers to predict quantitative changes in crime rates resulting from changes in exogenous variables. For example, predicted fluctuations in unemployment rates or in the age distribution of the population could be used to derive predictions of changes in property crime rates, other things equal. Forecasting requires estimating and solving the entire model. Thus the police production functions and the community demand equation would have to be estimated. In turn, estimating these equations illuminates some interesting issues. For example, the substitution of capital and labour inputs is of vital importance for the efficient allocation of resources within the police agency. The relationship between these inputs could be determined in estimating the police production functions.

More work needs to be done on the identification problem discussed in chapters 2 and 5. Recall that the difficulty is that recorded and actual crime rates may differ, thus making identification of the 'true' elasticities of the independent variables difficult. In chapter 5, a method for estimating the range of the true elasticities was presented, but different ranges would be forthcoming from different assumptions on the recording function. Information on recording ratios would permit estimation of the recording function using regression techniques. The estimated elasticities could then be used to determine the 'true' offence elasticities as discussed in chapter 2. The difficulty, of course, is obtaining a data base of recording ratios. Sample survey techniques may be required.

The efficiency of the allocation of resources within the criminal justice system also needs to be investigated. To do so, the over-all effects of changes in the crime control variables on crime rates must be estimated. In this study, only deterrent effects on prospective offenders have been estimated. Thus, one should not immediately infer, for example, that since longer expected sentences do not appear to deter prospective offenders, society would effect an efficiency gain by reducing sentences. The inference may not be justified, because sentences also serve to remove offenders from society and to change the expected returns from legitimate and criminal behaviour for released offenders. Thus, incarceration has functions other than the pure deterrent effect on prospective offenders, and the cost and benefits of these other functions must be investigated before an efficient allocation of resources could be determined. In turn, these investigations require adequate follow-up studies of released offenders.

Derivation of expected sentence lengths

In this appendix the unsuitability of a commonly used proxy for expected sentence lengths is first established, and then a detailed discussion of the proxy used in this study is presented.

Previous research on crime has used 'average sentence length served' as a proxy for expected sentence length. This variable is calculated as a weighted average of sentences served by releasees for a given year, the weights being equal to the proportion of releasees who have served a given sentence length. Table A.1 gives an example illustrating why the use of this variable can be expected to lead to spurious results, even if sentences do not change over time.

As indicated, thirty offenders are sentenced in every period (including t - 1 and t - 2) except t + 1 and t + 5. The crucial assumption underlying the example is that the actual distribution of sentences handed down by the courts does not change from period to period; exactly one-third of the number sentenced in each period receive (and serve) one-year sentences, one-third receive two-year sentences, and one-third receive three-year sentences. Thus, there is no change in expected sentence length served for any prospective offender contemplating a crime. However, as indicated in the right-most column of the table, the calculated proxy variable does change over time, simply because the number of offenders subjected to incarceration changes. For example, in period t + 1 the weights applied to the longer incarcerations increase because no offenders sentenced at the beginning of the period are released at the end. Furthermore, any change in the number sentenced has an effect not only on the weights used to calculate the average sentence length served for the current period but also on

TABLE A.1

Relationship between number of offences and average sentence length served

Period	Number sentenced	Number released by sentence length			Calculated average sentence length served
		1 yr	2 yrs	3 yrs	
t	30	10	10	10	$\frac{10}{30}\cdot1 + \frac{10}{30}\cdot2 + \frac{10}{30}\cdot3 = 2$
$t + 1$	0	0	10	10	$\frac{0}{20}\cdot1 + \frac{10}{20}\cdot2 + \frac{10}{20}\cdot3 = 2\frac{1}{2}$
$t + 2$	30	10	0	10	$\frac{10}{20}\cdot1 + \frac{0}{20}\cdot2 + \frac{10}{20}\cdot3 = 2$
$t + 3$	30	10	10	0	$\frac{10}{20}\cdot1 + \frac{10}{20}\cdot2 + \frac{0}{20}\cdot3 = 1\frac{1}{2}$
$t + 4$	30	10	10	10	$\frac{10}{30}\cdot1 + \frac{10}{30}\cdot2 + \frac{10}{30}\cdot3 = 2$
$t + 5$	60	20	10	10	$\frac{20}{40}\cdot1 + \frac{10}{40}\cdot2 + \frac{10}{40}\cdot3 = 1\frac{3}{4}$
$t + 6$	30	10	20	10	$\frac{10}{40}\cdot1 + \frac{20}{40}\cdot2 + \frac{10}{40}\cdot3 = 2$
$t + 7$	30	10	10	20	$\frac{10}{40}\cdot1 + \frac{10}{40}\cdot2 + \frac{20}{40}\cdot3 = 2\frac{1}{4}$
$t + 8$	30	10	10	10	$\frac{10}{30}\cdot1 + \frac{10}{30}\cdot2 + \frac{10}{30}\cdot3 = 2$

the weights used in the succeeding two periods. In actuality, since the number sentenced tends to increase over time the calculated sentence length variable would tend to decrease, other things equal. To summarize: a simple change in the number of offenders sentenced will change the calculated variable commonly used as a proxy for the anticipated severity of sentences, even though there is no actual change in the sentencing behaviour of the courts.

An alternative method was adopted in this paper. A proxy for expected sentence lengths was generated by utilizing judicial data on sentences handed down. These data, available by crime, by province, and by year, were 'corrected' to reflect parole and remission possibilities. A detailed explanation of the derivation of the proxy variable follows.

Column 1 of Table A.2 lists the relevant categories of judicial sentences published by Statistics Canada. These data are converted into specific monthly sentences in column 2. The following procedure was used to derive column 2: 1/ A sentence length of zero was applied to all sentence categories not involving prison sentences. In effect, no distinction was made between fines, suspended sentences, and no penalty. Data limitations on the amounts of fines and on probation conditions preclude assigning non-zero values to these sentences. 2/ The midpoint is utilized for every sentence category that spans a time interval with fixed endpoints. 3/ For open-ended sentences (indefinite or definite sentences categorized without end-points by Statistics Canada), column 2 lists the lower bound of the sentence. 4/ Twenty-one years was arbitrarily taken as the sentence length for the sentence categories 'life' and 'preventive detention.' 5/ Six months was arbitrarily taken as the sentence length for sentence categories 'training school' and 'indefinite term only.'

To correct for parole and remissions it was first noted that an offender is released from custody either on parole or by virtue of the expiry of sentence. In the latter case, an offender can be released early because of statutory and earned remissions. Statutory remission is one-quarter of the sentence handed down, and earned remissions are three days for each month served (approximately one-tenth of the sentence). Thus the 'remission factor' in column 4, where applicable, was $0.9 \times 0.75 = 0.68$; that is, the representative offender who expects to be released by virtue of expiry of sentence anticipates serving 68 per cent of his sentence in custody.

Parole regulations state that an offender serving a definite sentence less than life may be paroled after serving one-third of the sentence or four years, whichever is less. However some sentences are so short that it is impossible to make a parole decision before the offender is released with remissions. Here it is assumed that offenders sentenced to six months or less are not able to obtain parole. (In discussions with the National Parole Board it was established that this approximates their general procedure, although parole has been awarded to short-term offenders in special circumstances.) Thus, 'parole factors' in column 3 are zero for short sentences and 0.33 for long sentences. For sentences greater than six months but less than fifteen, factors were chosen to yield a five-month incarceration, one month to apply and four months to process the application.

A final piece of information relates to the expectation of release by parole vs expiry. Table A.3 contains information on prisoners released by type of release for penitentiaries. These data are available by crime for each year, but not by province; it is assumed that the true figures for each province are the national figures for penitentiaries.

TABLE A.2

Average sentence lengths, parole factors, and remission factors used in calculating
the average sentence length variable

Sentence category	Sentence (months)	Parole factor	Remission factor
(1)	(2)	(3)	(4)
Suspended sentence without probation	0	0	0
Suspended sentence with probation	0	0	0
Fine	0	0	0
Jail			
Under 1 month	0.5	0	0.68
1 month and under 2	1.5	0	0.68
2 months and under 3	2.5	0	0.68
3 months and under 6	4.5	0	0.68
6 months exact	6.0	0	0.68
Over 6 months and under 9	7.5	0.67	0.68
9 months and under 12	10.5	0.48	0.68
12 months and under 15	13.5	0.37	0.68
15 months and under 18	16.5	0.33	0.68
18 months and under 21	19.5	0.33	0.68
21 months and under 24	22.5	0.33	0.68
Reformatory, definite term[1]			
Under 1 month	0.5	0	0.68
1 month and under 2	1.5	0	0.68
2 months and under 3	2.5	0	0.68
3 months and under 6	4.0	0	0.68
6 months exact	6.0	0	0.68
Over 6 months and under 9	7.5	0.67	0.68
9 months and under 12	10.5	0.48	0.68
12 months and under 15	13.5	0.37	0.68
15 months and under 18	16.5	0.33	0.68
18 months and under 21	19.5	0.33	0.68
21 months and under 24	22.5	0.33	0.68
24 months and over	24.0	0.33	0.68
Reformatory, definite and indefinite terms[2]			
3 months and under 6 and indef. term	4.5	0	0.68
6 months exact and indef. term	6.0	0	0.68
Over 6 months and under 9 and indef. term	7.5	0.67	0.68
9 months and under 12 and indef. term	10.5	0.48	0.68
12 months and under 15 and indef. term	13.5	0.37	0.68
15 months and under 18 and indef. term	16.5	0.33	0.68
18 months and under 21 and indef. term	19.5	0.33	0.68
21 months and under 24 and indef. term	22.5	0.33	0.68

TABLE A.2 continued

Sentence category	Sentence (months)	Parole factor	Remission factor
(1)	(2)	(3)	(4)
Indef. term only[3]	6.0	0	0
Training School	6.0	0	0
Penitentiary			
Under 2 years	12.0	0.42	0.68
2 years and under 5	42.0	0.33	0.68
5 years and under 10	90.0	0.33	0.68
10 years and under 14	144.0	0.33	0.68
14 years and over	178.0	0.29	0.68
Life	252.0	0.33	0
Preventive detention	252.0	0.33	0

NOTE: Sentence, Parole factor, and Remission factor: see text for derivation
1 Female persons in Nova Scotia and New Brunswick only
2 Persons in Ontario only
3 Female persons committed to Vanier Institute in Ontario only
SOURCE: Tables 6A, 6B, and 7, *Statistics of Criminal and Other Offences,* Statistics Canada, Cat. 85-201 (Annual)

TABLE A.3

Persons released from prison on parole or whose sentence expired, percentage by crime type and year

		1970	1971	1972
Robbery	paroled	0.69	0.70	0.78
	expired	0.31	0.30	0.22
Break and enter	paroled	0.62	0.61	0.73
	expired	0.38	0.39	0.29
Theft	paroled	0.59	0,54	0.74
	expired	0.41	0.46	0.26
Have stolen goods	paroled	0.57	0.58	0.78
	expired	0.43	0.42	0.22
Fraud	paroled	0.56	0.61	0.72
	expired	0.44	0.39	0.28

SOURCE: *Correctional Institution Statistics,* Statistics Canada, Cat. 85-207 (Annual) Table 19

The expected sentence length for each observation, that is, for each provi
and each year, by crime type may now be calculated. The formula is

$$\mathrm{ES}_{i,j,t} = \sum_{r=1}^{43} (N_{i,j,t}^r \, / \sum_{r=1}^{43} N_{i,j,t}^r) \, [\mathrm{PF}^r \cdot \mathrm{PP}_{i,t} + \mathrm{RF}^r \cdot \mathrm{PR}_{i,t}] \cdot S^r,$$

where $\mathrm{ES}_{i,j,t}$ is the expected sentence length for crime type i in province j and
for year t; $N_{i,j,t}^r$ is the number of offenders sentenced to the rth sentence category for crime type i, province j, and year t; PF^r is the 'parole factor' for the rth
sentence category (see column 3 of Table A.2); $\mathrm{PP}_{i,t}$ is the percentage of releasees
from penitentiaries that receive a paroled release, for crime type i and in year t
(see Table A.3); RF^r is the 'remission factor' for the rth sentence category (see
column 4 of Table A.2); $\mathrm{PR}_{i,t}$ is the percentage of releasees from penitentiaries
that receive a release due to expiry of sentence (i.e. receive remissions) for crime
type i and in year t (see Table A.3); and S^r is the sentence, in months, for the rth
sentence category (see column 2 of Table A.2).

Some rather important limitations of the variable ES as calculated above
should be mentioned. First, in the selection of parole and remission factors
(columns 3 and 4 of Table A.2) and the assignment of sentence 'points' (column
2 of Table A.2), an implicit assumption of optimism is made. Thus, for example,
the prospective offender assumes that if he is paroled he will receive parole at
the earliest possible date. Second, it is implicitly assumed that all information
bearing on the formulation of expected sentence lengths comes from the current
period. Thus, for example, the prospective offender looks only at judicial sentencing practices for the current year. This appears to be a rather limiting assumption; the use of distributed lags may be justified. Unfortunately, the necessary
data for sentence lengths are not available for 1969. Third, a prospective offender's expectations may depend upon his previous record; it is impossible to
account for this phenomenon in the derivation of the expected sentence length
variable.

Police and judicial crime classifications

The following classifications and Criminal Code specifications pertain to 1970, 1971 and 1972.

ROBBERY

The police classify only Robbery, whereas the courts distinguish between Robbery and Robbery while armed.

BREAKING AND ENTERING

The police classify only Breaking and entering, whereas the courts distinguish between Breaking and entering a place and Breaking and entering while armed. Violations of sections 309, 310, and 311 of the Criminal Code are included in the judicial classification but excluded from the police classification. These sections are as follows: 309 Possession of any instrument suitable for house-breaking or safebreaking *or* having one's face disguised under suspicious circumstances; 310 Possession of instruments for breaking into a coin-operated device; 311 Selling or advertising an automobile master key without a licence.

THEFT A

The police distinguish between Theft under fifty dollars and Theft over fifty dollars, whereas the courts separate Theft and Theft by conversion. Violations of

Criminal Code sections 285, 287, 288, 289, and 291, listed below, are included in the judicial classification, but excluded from the police classification: 285 Failure to deliver goods under seizure; 287 Using or diverting electricity, gas or telecommunication services without right; 288 Theft by or from person having special interest, e.g. by a lessee, by one of several joint owners, by directors of a company; 287 Theft by spouse while intending to desert or on deserting or while living apart; also assisting or receiving goods obtained as above; 291 Theft by person holding power of attorney. Included in judicial 'theft' is actual theft of motor vehicles; this is not included in police data.

THEFT B

Police data distinguish between Theft of motor vehicle, Theft under fifty dollars, and Theft over fifty dollars, whereas the courts classify Taking motor vehicle without consent (a summary offence only), Theft, and Theft by conversion. Violations of Criminal Code sections 285, 287, 288, and 291, specified above, are included in the judicial classification, but excluded from the police classification. In police data, 'theft of motor vehicle' includes both joy-riding and 'car rings.'

FRAUD

Police data classify only fraud. Court data specify Trade mark contravention, Indecent telephone calling, and Fraudulently obtaining transportation (summary and indictable offences); Impersonation at examination, Fraudulently obtaining food and lodging, Falsification of employment record, and Obtaining carriage by false billing (summary offences only); False pretences, Forging and uttering, and Fraud and corruption. The following violations of Criminal Code Sections are excluded from police information but listed in judicial data, although impossible to separate under single listings: 58 False statement to procure passport, possession of forged passport, 59 Fraudulent use of certificate of citizenship (58 and 59 being included in judicial 'false pretences'), 108-14 Bribery, government corruption, etc. (included in judicial 'fraud and corruption'), 127 Obstructing justice, 130 Corruptly taking reward for recovery of goods, 192 Cheating at play, 297 Public servant refusing to deliver property, 299 Taking possession of drift timber, 300 Destroying documents of title to goods or lands, 301 Fraudulently removing or concealing, 373 Offences in relation to a wreck, 375 Applying or removing 'distinguishing marks' without authority, 376 Selling defective stores to Her Majesty, 378 Buying or receiving military stores, 383 Bribing an employee or deceiving an employer. The following two violations are included in police 'fraud' but not in the judicial data: 371 Falsely claiming that goods are made for Her Majesty, 323 Pretending to practise witchcraft.

NOTE: These classifications are based primarily on Cassidy, Hopkinson, and Laycock (1973), and also on the *Uniform Crime Reporting Manual* (1974) and the Criminal Code of Canada.

Two-stage least squares regression estimates of the supply-of-offences equations

The estimates in this appendix assume that both the probability of apprehension and the expected sentence length variables are endogenous. These assumptions are justified if the courts respond to higher recorded offence rates by imposing longer sentences on convicted criminals. This phenomena can be accounted for by adding the equations

$$S_i = j_i(O_i), \quad (i = 1, ..., n),$$

to the model specified in the text; the estimated coefficient of O_i is predicted to be positive. It is recognized that bounds on sentence lengths are determined by statute. However, the specified equations allow for the fact that sentencing agents have wide latitude within the statutory limits.

Tables C.1 to C.4 of this appendix present the estimated elasticities of the supply-of-offences function under the assumption that the equations specified above are a part of the model presented in the text. A comparison of the expected sentence length elasticities in Tables 7 to 10 with those reported in this appendix indicates some support for the hypothesis. If the hypothesis is correct, any positive relationship between offence rates and sentence lengths due to sentencing behaviour should be removed. In no case are the results perverse in the sense that a reported insignificant elasticity in Tables 7 to 10 becomes positive significant in Tables C.1 to C.4. For two crimes in several equations, a positive significant elasticity in Tables 7 to 10 becomes insignificant in Tables C.1 to C.4 (break and enter, Tables 9 and C.3; robbery, Tables 9 and C.3). In one equation for fraud a previously insignificant elasticity becomes negative significant (fraud, Tables 9 and C.3). These results are in agreement with the hypothesis.

TABLE C.1

Regression estimates of the offence equations: two-stage least squares, clearance rate and sentence length endogenous

Intercept	ln $\hat{P}$	ln Q	ln $\hat{S}$	ln DIST	ln VS	R^2
Theft A						
−3.119	−0.756	−1.843	0.030	1.321	0.185	0.980
(−10.643)	(−4.375)	(−4.181)	(0.735)	(11.557)	(11.739)	
Theft B						
−3.241	−0.776	−1.568	0.978	1.419	0.182	0.981
(−11.034)	(−4.444)	(−3.513)	(2.219)	(14.287)	(12.182)	
Fraud						
−11.774	−1.095	−0.616	−0.040	3.538	0.338	0.922
(−7.949)	(−1.755)	(−0.406)	(−1.480)	(8.403)	(6.206)	
Break and enter						
−4.568	−1.530	0.214	0.130	1.404	0.074	0.919
(−3.945)	(−4.809)	(0.178)	(0.641)	(5.457)	(1.827)	
Robbery						
−9.139	−0.734	−3.063	0.659	1.103	0.270	0.897
(5.254)	(−2.210)	(−5.290)	(4.544)	(2.196)	(3.999)	

NOTE: Numbers in parentheses are t-values.

However, due to the tenuousness of the evidence the material is relegated to an appendix, and the hypothesis remains a suitable topic for future research.

TABLE C.2

Regression estimates of the offence equations including Indian and age variables: clearance rate and sentence length endogenous

Intercept	ln $\hat{P}$	ln Q	ln $\hat{S}$	ln DIST	ln VS	ln IND	ln A_{15-24}	R^2
Theft A								
-2.498 (-5.300)	-0.709 (-4.232)	-1.893 (-4.481)	-0.016 (-0.341)	1.157 (7.814)	0.166 (8.731)	0.038 (1.639)		0.982
-2.735 (-4.373)	-0.857 (-3.722)	-1.862 (-4.050)	0.036 (0.827)	1.358 (10.442)	0.192 (9.875)		0.403 (0.705)	0.979
-2.441 (-3.873)	-0.732 (-3.098)	-1.895 (-4.330)	-0.013 (-0.249)	1.171 (6.451)	0.168 (6.661)	0.037 (1.406)	0.084 (0.143)	0.982
Theft B								
-2.711 (-5.923)	-0.773 (-4.574)	-1.587 (-3.671)	0.033 (0.717)	1.264 (8.882)	0.164 (8.776)	0.033 (1.479)		0.983
-3.011 (-5.453)	-0.845 (-3.700)	-1.552 (-3.342)	0.085 (2.175)	1.453 (11.786)	0.187 (10.049)		0.268 (0.500)	0.980
-2.649 (-4.428)	-0.797 (-3.563)	-1.581 (-3.519)	0.036 (0.699)	1.280 (7.298)	0.166 (7.064)	0.032 (1.341)	0.091 (0.171)	0.983
Fraud								
-11.311 (-5.403)	-0.974 (-1.315)	-0.397 (-0.235)	-0.040 (-1.458)	3.407 (5.729)	0.337 (6.088)	0.021 (0.319)		0.924
-13.514 (-10.384)	-0.738 (-1.608)	-0.277 (-0.263)	-0.001 (-0.057)	3.157 (9.308)	0.259 (4.954)		-2.074 (-2.138)	0.965
-15.807 (-6.500)	-0.966 (-1.872)	-0.829 (-0.696)	0.016 (0.530)	3.407 (8.220)	0.225 (3.612)	-0.068 (-1.132)	-3.026 (-2.311)	0.965

TABLE C.2 continued

Intercept	ln $\hat{P}$	ln Q	ln $\hat{S}$	ln DIST	ln VS	ln IND	ln $A_{15\text{-}24}$	R^2
Break and enter								
-3.799	-1.329	-0.144	0.089	1.236	0.073	0.025		0.925
(-1.944)	(-2.559)	(-0.103)	(0.411)	(2.889)	(1.816)	(0.486)		
-3.742	-1.716	0.081	0.119	1.541	0.077		0.887	0.916
(-2.568)	(-4.517)	(0.064)	(0.560)	(5.115)	(1.815)		(1.029)	
-3.452	-1.620	-0.066	0.102	1.462	0.076	0.011	0.842	0.919
(-1.627)	(-2.544)	(-0.044)	(0.440)	(2.826)	(1.780)	(0.189)	(0.933)	
Robbery								
-6.422	-0.795	-2.154	0.499	0.451	0.223	0.235		0.951
(-4.267)	(-3.371)	(-4.294)	(4.350)	(1.096)	(4.462)	(3.135)		
-11.585	-0.583	-2.950	0.462	0.553	0.203		-3.046	0.930
(-5.189)	(-1.945)	(-5.945)	(2.533)	(0.974)	(2.762)		(-1.459)	
-8.526	-0.670	-2.111	0.349	0.044	0.172	0.223	-2.445	0.969
(-4.845)	(-3.223)	(-5.092)	(2.691)	(0.105)	(3.345)	(3.579)	(-1.687)	

NOTE: Numbers in parentheses are t-values.

TABLE C.3

Regression estimates of the offence equations including Indian, age, and labour force activity variables: two-stage least squares, clearance rate and sentence length endogenous

Intercept	$\ln \hat{P}$	$\ln Q$	$\ln \hat{S}$	$\ln$ DIST	$\ln$ VS	$\ln$ UN	$\ln$ PR	$\ln$ IND	$\ln A_{15\text{-}24}$	R^2
Theft A										
-0.442	-0.857	-1.504	0.200	1.628	0.263	0.106	-1.067			0.986
(-0.324)	(-5.809)	(-3.599)	(3.022)	(11.488)	(8.859)	(1.873)	(-2.421)			
-1.064	-0.756	-1.431	0.129	1.392	0.231	0.153	-0.686	0.047		0.991
(-0.881)	(-5.594)	(-3.963)	(1.977)	(8.582)	(7.842)	(2.886)	(-1.645)	(2.198)		
-0.448	-0.849	-1.501	0.200	1.627	0.263	0.106	-1.077		-0.037	0.986
(-0.318)	(-4.504)	(-3.468)	(2.912)	(11.097)	(8.599)	(1.816)	(-2.261)		(-0.072)	
-1.267	-0.631	-1.373	0.125	1.332	0.224	0.169	-0.745	0.056	-0.479	0.992
(-1.086)	(-3.652)	(-3.941)	(2.002)	(8.103)	(7.762)	(3.206)	(-1.858)	(2.543)	(-1.078)	
Theft B										
-1.024	-0.856	-1.322	0.210	1.666	0.243	0.077	-0.868			0.986
(-0.721)	(-5.050)	(-3.053)	(3.156)	(11.815)	(8.107)	(1.342)	(-1.879)			
-1.695	-0.764	-1.257	0.136	1.418	0.211	0.131	-0.473	0.047		0.989
(-1.295)	(-4.846)	(-3.236)	(1.979)	(8.283)	(6.873)	(2.294)	(-1.045)	(2.141)		
-1.094	-0.813	-1.315	0.212	1.656	0.243	0.082	-0.905		-0.180	0.986
(-0.747)	(-3.856)	(-2.973)	(3.112)	(11.292)	(7.924)	(1.363)	(-1.875)		(-0.358)	
-2.022	-0.620	-1.224	0.129	1.343	0.204	0.156	-0.512	0.055	-0.533	0.991
(-1.563)	(-3.183)	(-3.256)	(1.939)	(7.592)	(6.756)	(2.642)	(-1.168)	(2.479)	(-1.187)	

TABLE C.3 continued

Intercept	$\ln \hat{P}$	$\ln Q$	$\ln \hat{S}$	$\ln$ DIST	$\ln$ VS	$\ln$ UN	$\ln$ PR	$\ln$ IND	$\ln A_{15-24}$	R^2
Fraud										
-13.637 (-3.671)	-1.039 (-1.793)	-0.470 (-0.294)	-0.034 (-1.537)	3.524 (8.654)	0.342 (5.824)	0.188 (1.066)	0.397 (0.461)			0.937
-2.644 (-0.280)	0.245 (0.190)	1.709 (0.550)	-0.111 (-1.807)	1.769 (1.359)	0.502 (3.510)	0.926 (1.677)	-1.427 (-0.757)	0.428 (1.614)		0.818
-11.741 (-4.384)	-0.847 (-2.062)	-1.192 (-1.042)	-0.016 (-0.964)	3.215 (10.606)	0.286 (6.352)	-0.130 (-3.049)	-1.061 (-1.039)		-3.140 (-1.378)	0.971
-3.650 (-0.415)	0.117 (0.098)	1.145 (0.363)	-0.094 (-1.295)	1.927 (1.563)	0.459 (2.681)	0.797 (1.322)	-1.640 (-0.927)	0.365 (1.247)	-1.042 (-0.367)	0.866
Break and enter										
-7.119 (-2.528)	-1.645 (-5.355)	0.993 (0.776)	0.260 (1.187)	1.552 (5.939)	0.088 (2.065)	0.161 (1.477)	0.377 (0.608)			0.928
-4.850 (-2.423)	-0.830 (-2.332)	-0.099 (-0.108)	0.199 (1.384)	0.901 (3.106)	0.106 (3.784)	0.361 (3.570)	0.422 (1.047)	0.132 (2.763)		0.972
-6.959 (-2.363)	-1.777 (-5.172)	0.905 (0.676)	0.246 (1.073)	1.667 (5.684)	0.086 (1.946)	0.151 (1.319)	0.651 (0.934)		1.026 (1.073)	0.926
-4.622 (-2.233)	-0.697 (-1.323)	-0.206 (-0.217)	0.195 (1.389)	0.792 (1.839)	0.109 (3.788)	0.388 (3.058)	0.353 (0.798)	0.148 (2.233)	-0.277 (-0.336)	0.975

TABLE C.3 continued

Intercept	$\ln \hat{P}$	$\ln Q$	$\ln \hat{S}$	$\ln$ DIST	$\ln$ VS	$\ln$ UN	$\ln$ PR	$\ln$ IND	$\ln A_{15\text{-}24}$	R^2
Robbery										
12.171	−1.138	−3.491	1.233	1.962	0.396	−0.936	−6.228			0.801
(0.623)	(−2.416)	(−3.015)	(1.889)	(1.563)	(1.912)	(−1.611)	(−1.018)			
7.978	−1.049	−2.904	1.002	1.393	0.347	−0.602	−4.638	0.136		0.871
(0.462)	(−2.553)	(−2.291)	(1.587)	(1.059)	(1.875)	(−0.893)	(−0.836)	(0.710)		
10.764	−1.081	−3.457	1.163	1.790	0.376	−0.886	−6.036		−0.843	0.822
(5.34)	(−2.023)	(−3.028)	(1.622)	(1.219)	(1.683)	(−1.444)	(−1.000)		(−0.213)	
3.644	−0.894	−2.665	0.781	0.846	0.288	−0.397	−3.765	0.173	−1.902	0.921
(0.235)	(−2.182)	(−2.437)	(1.268)	(0.623)	(1.640)	(−0.629)	(−0.800)	(1.046)	(−0.652)	

NOTE: Numbers in parentheses are t-values.

TABLE C.4

Regression estimates of the offence equations, including Indian, age, and labour force activity (males aged fourteen to twenty-four) variables: two-stage least squares, clearance rate and sentence length endogenous

Intercept	$\ln \hat{P}$	$\ln Q$	$\ln \hat{S}$	$\ln$ DIST	$\ln$ VS	$\ln UN_{14\text{-}24}$	$\ln PR_{14\text{-}24}$	$\ln$ IND	$\ln A_{15\text{-}24}$	R^2
Theft A										
−3.972 (−3.050)	−0.764 (−4.161)	−1.427 (−2.851)	0.097 (1.857)	1.455 (9.797)	0.212 (10.257)	0.126 (1.647)	0.010 (0.028)			0.983
−3.018 (−2.808)	−0.721 (−4.937)	−1.329 (−3.344)	0.061 (1.417)	1.280 (9.843)	0.196 (11.361)	0.181 (2.870)	−0.100 (−0.352)	0.063 (3.143)		0.990
−3.844 (−2.791)	−0.820 (−3.688)	−1.434 (−2.759)	0.098 (1.800)	1.467 (9.400)	0.217 (9.329)	0.127 (1.600)	0.059 (0.155)		0.280 (0.491)	0.983
−3.075 (−2.994)	−0.596 (−3.415)	−1.293 (−3.397)	0.052 (1.241)	1.218 (9.052)	0.183 (9.394)	0.190 (3.139)	−0.225 (−0.776)	0.076 (3.436)	−0.576 (−1.191)	0.992
Theft B										
−4.398 (−3.423)	−0.722 (−3.716)	−1.191 (−2.432)	0.134 (2.670)	1.513 (10.558)	0.207 (10.117)	0.126 (1.634)	0.135 (0.383)			0.984
−3.402 (−2.964)	−0.747 (−4.526)	−1.085 (−2.612)	0.099 (2.231)	1.358 (10.123)	0.191 (10.459)	0.169 (2.674)	−0.015 (−2.517)	−0.055 (−0.048)		0.989
−4.331 (−3.178)	−0.753 (−3.197)	−1.188 (−2.342)	0.135 (2.585)	1.521 (10.002)	0.208 (9.313)	0.124 (1.556)	0.155 (0.412)		0.127 (0.232)	0.984
−3.484 (−3.113)	−0.648 (−3.405)	−1.077 (−2.664)	0.091 (2.067)	1.305 (9.218)	0.182 (9.138)	0.181 (2.724)	−0.112 (−0.358)	0.064 (2.902)	−0.468 (−0.973)	0.990

TABLE C.4 continued

Intercept	ln $\hat{P}$	ln Q	ln $\hat{S}$	ln DIST	ln VS	ln $UN_{14\text{-}24}$	ln $PR_{14\text{-}24}$	ln IND	ln $A_{15\text{-}24}$	R^2
Fraud										
-16.752	-0.624	0.612	-0.009	3.079	0.345	0.294	1.441			0.961
(-6.085)	(-1.636)	(0.472)	(-0.706)	(9.518)	(8.218)	(1.969)	(2.184)			
-6.820	0.603	1.461	-0.058	2.039	0.408	0.696	-0.425	0.327		0.927
(-0.753)	(0.526)	(0.744)	(-1.313)	(2.100)	(5.162)	(0.393)	(-1.799)	(2.690)		
-15.544	-0.743	-0.321	-0.006	3.181	0.275	0.223	0.180		-2.418	0.972
(-6.264)	(-2.185)	(-0.264)	(-0.552)	(11.034)	(5.681)	(1.650)	(0.223)		(-2.256)	
-4.423	0.609	0.544	-0.061	2.036	0.339	0.663	-1.996	0.363	-2.621	0.936
(-0.496)	(0.548)	(0.272)	(-1.410)	(2.161)	(3.822)	(1.737)	(-0.991)	(1.383)	(-1.560)	
Break and enter										
-9.772	-1.515	1.734	0.390	1.518	0.128	0.272	0.910			0.941
(-3.393)	(-4.665)	(1.493)	(2.063)	(5.933)	(2.980)	(2.204)	(1.366)			
-7.105	-0.864	0.527	0.291	1.007	0.132	0.399	0.742	0.111		0.971
(-3.009)	(-2.396)	(0.538)	(2.043)	(3.557)	(4.272)	(3.842)	(1.526)	(2.376)		
-9.735	-1.617	1.755	0.399	1.596	0.141	0.279	1.242		1.100	0.943
(-3.333)	(-4.779)	(1.490)	(2.080)	(5.995)	(3.158)	(2.225)	(1.720)		(1.307)	
-7.157	-0.880	0.552	0.293	1.020	0.133	0.397	0.756	0.108	0.038	0.971
(-2.556)	(-1.552)	(0.458)	(1.840)	(2.300)	(3.962)	(3.216)	(1.199)	(1.448)	(0.039)	

TABLE C.4 continued

Intercept	ln $\hat{P}$	ln Q	ln $\hat{S}$	ln DIST	ln VS	ln UN$_{14\text{-}24}$	ln PR$_{14\text{-}24}$	ln IND	ln $A_{15\text{-}24}$	R^2
Robbery										
-18.357 (-2.367)	-0.846 (-3.705)	-2.114 (-3.675)	0.191 (0.748)	-0.259 (-0.342)	0.218 (4.492)	-0.022 (-0.067)	3.666 (1.539)			0.960
-11.578 (-1.458)	-0.783 (-3.621)	-1.905 (-3.474)	0.304 (1.236)	-0.047 (-0.066)	0.217 (4.776)	0.086 (0.281)	1.726 (0.715)	1.000 (2.126)		0.967
-17.677 (-2.243)	-0.760 (-2.946)	-2.233 (-3.706)	0.189 (0.730)	-0.260 (-0.341)	0.196 (3.418)	-0.032 (-0.098)	2.987 (1.160)		-1.365 (-0.737)	0.962
-7.624 (-0.904)	-0.556 (-2.163)	-2.118 (-3.693)	0.336 (1.335)	0.023 (0.031)	0.165 (2.955)	0.098 (0.313)	-0.563 (-0.201)	0.269 (2.582)	-3.250 (-1.713)	0.968

NOTE: Numbers in parentheses are t-values.

APPENDIX D

Ordinary least squares estimates of the supply-of-offences equations

TABLE D.1

Regression estimates of the offence equations: ordinary least squares

Intercept	ln P	ln Q	ln S	ln DIST	ln VS	R^2
Theft A						
−3.108	−0.669	−1.896	0.042	1.353	0.188	0.980
(−10.770)	(−4.894)	(−4.389)	(1.211)	(12.929)	(12.516)	
Theft B						
−3.190	−0.669	−1.665	0.082	1.432	0.183	0.981
(−11.073)	(−4.837)	(−3.833)	(2.579)	(15.114)	(12.765)	
Fraud						
−11.401	1.682	−0.144	−0.031	3.063	0.466	0.758
(−3.718)	(2.770)	(−0.054)	(−1.305)	(3.740)	(5.037)	
Break and enter						
−4.412	−1.280	0.161	0.207	1.370	0.102	0.925
(−4.788)	(−5.146)	(0.171)	(1.419)	(6.343)	(3.168)	
Robbery						
−9.139	−0.764	−2.870	0.483	0.861	0.282	0.914
(−5.254)	(−3.210)	(−5.606)	(4.464)	(1.920)	(4.613)	

NOTE: Numbers in parentheses are t-values.

TABLE D.2

Regression estimates of the offence equations including Indian and age variables: ordinary least squares

	Intercept	ln P	ln Q	ln S	ln DIST	ln VS	ln IND	ln A_{15-24}	R^2
Theft A									
	-2.502	-0.618	-1.932	0.000	1.196	0.167	0.038		0.983
	(-5.541)	(-4.631)	(-4.692)	(0.001)	(8.771)	(9.486)	(1.691)		
	-2.951	-0.699	-1.910	0.046	1.372	0.191		0.163	0.980
	(-5.110)	(-4.150)	(-4.288)	(1.219)	(11.134)	(10.217)		(0.317)	
	-2.578	-0.598	-1.924	-0.004	1.177	0.167	0.039	-0.104	0.983
	(-4.312)	(-3.466)	(-4.520)	(-0.089)	(6.990)	(7.128)	(1.621)	(-0.201)	
Theft B									
	-2.662	-0.679	-1.684	0.041	1.284	0.167	0.033		0.983
	(-6.053)	(-4.861)	(-4.025)	(1.025)	(9.730)	(9.539)	(1.549)		
	-3.147	-0.709	-1.665	0.083	1.439	0.184		0.049	0.981
	(-5.930)	(-3.969)	(-3.727)	(2.307)	(12.065)	(10.233)		(0.098)	
	-2.747	-0.655	-1.685	0.036	1.263	0.164	0.034	-0.117	0.983
	(-4.776)	(-3.733)	(-3.912)	(0.774)	(7.744)	(7.437)	(1.521)	(-0.239)	
Fraud									
	-7.301	1.711	1.696	-0.028	2.011	0.414	0.176		0.799
	(-2.009)	(2.999)	(0.631)	(-1.263)	(2.103)	(4.536)	(1.850)		
	-13.656	-0.776	-0.242	0.001	3.172	0.255		-2.136	0.966
	(-11.250)	(-2.489)	(-0.233)	(0.082)	(12.242)	(6.098)		(-2.892)	
	-15.204	-0.979	-0.768	0.004	3.405	0.243	-0.054	-2.611	0.968
	(-8.368)	(-2.742)	(-0.680)	(0.441)	(10.375)	(5.694)	(-1.137)	(-3.097)	

TABLE D.2 continued

Intercept	ln P	ln Q	ln S	ln DIST	ln VS	ln IND	ln A_{15-24}	R^2
Break and enter								
−3.322 (−2.552)	−1.034 (−3.199)	−0.186 (0.190)	0.158 (1.052)	1.126 (3.778)	0.096 (2.953)	0.046 (1.173)		0.931
−3.969 (−3.247)	−1.340 (−4.875)	0.066 (0.068)	0.206 (1.385)	1.429 (5.868)	0.106 (3.155)		0.431 (0.565)	0.927
−2.921 (−1.914)	−1.094 (−3.138)	−0.271 (−0.268)	0.158 (1.027)	1.185 (3.662)	0.100 (2.937)	0.045 (1.132)	0.406 (0.536)	0.932
Robbery								
−5.186 (−4.157)	−0.783 (−4.661)	−1.885 (−4.429)	0.358 (4.395)	0.178 (0.504)	0.223 (4.916)	0.282 (4.378)		0.960
3.093 (4.268)	−0.528 (−2.234)	−1.063 (−4.538)	0.009 (2.090)	0.004 (0.388)	−0.000 (−0.388)		−9.983 (−2.944)	0.852
2.692 (2.810)	−0.597 (−2.275)	−0.963 (−3.410)	0.011 (2.146)	0.002 (0.153)	−0.000 (−0.002)	0.018 (0.656)	−8.231 (−1.886)	0.856

NOTE: Numbers in parentheses are t-values.

TABLE D.3

Regression estimates of the offence equations including Indian, age, and labour force activity variables: ordinary least squares

Intercept	ln P	ln Q	ln S	ln DIST	ln VS	ln UN	ln PR	ln IND	ln $A_{15\text{-}24}$	R^2
Theft A										
-0.810 (-0.624)	-0.763 (-6.214)	-1.602 (-3.961)	0.188 (3.184)	1.617 (12.468)	0.256 (9.384)	0.098 (1.810)	-0.924 (-2.246)			0.987
-1.316 (-1.160)	-0.673 (-6.040)	-1.483 (-4.219)	0.120 (2.096)	1.372 (9.340)	0.225 (8.522)	0.156 (3.005)	-0.574 (-1.513)	0.052 (2.563)		0.991
-0.839 (-0.630)	-0.729 (-5.027)	-1.575 (-3.764)	0.191 (3.136)	1.606 (11.898)	0.255 (9.113)	0.101 (1.800)	-0.989 (-2.231)		-0.222 (-0.476)	0.987
-1.486 (-1.355)	-0.565 (-4.376)	-1.389 (-4.042)	0.115 (2.074)	1.298 (8.665)	0.218 (8.392)	0.173 (3.376)	-0.683 (-1.834)	0.062 (2.998)	-0.591 (-1.493)	0.992
Theft B										
-1.235 (-0.990)	-0.791 (-5.464)	-1.385 (-3.270)	0.207 (3.405)	1.663 (12.595)	0.241 (8.595)	0.079 (1.431)	-0.790 (-1.796)			0.986
-1.773 (-1.419)	-0.707 (-5.254)	-1.291 (-3.390)	0.141 (2.284)	1.427 (9.024)	0.213 (7.541)	0.137 (2.460)	-0.445 (-1.054)	0.048 (2.245)		0.989
-1.324 (-0.939)	-0.743 (-4.407)	-1.364 (-3.141)	0.208 (3.348)	1.642 (11.791)	0.240 (8.343)	0.085 (1.480)	-0.852 (-1.845)		-0.272 (-0.582)	0.986
-2.052 (-1.668)	-0.593 (-3.842)	-1.230 (-3.303)	0.131 (2.180)	1.343 (8.141)	0.204 (7.331)	0.159 (2.820)	-0.514 (-1.244)	0.056 (2.605)	-0.572 (-1.381)	0.991

TABLE D.3 continued

Intercept	ln P	ln Q	ln S	ln DIST	ln VS	ln UN	ln PR	ln IND	ln A_{15-24}	R^2
Fraud										
−32.029	1.199	2.640	−0.033	4.042	0.421	0.618	4.086			0.836
(−4.032)	(2.148)	(1.032)	(−1.500)	(4.960)	(0.090)	(2.042)	(2.737)			
−15.663	1.437	3.438	−0.048	2.178	0.450	0.838	1.516	0.302		0.867
(−1.357)	(2.679)	(1.419)	(−2.162)	(1.725)	(5.268)	(2.737)	(0.771)	(1.848)		
−11.833	−0.811	−1.078	−0.002	3.168	0.264	0.100	−1.084		−3.446	0.975
(−4.950)	(−2.821)	(−1.023)	(−0.223)	(13.355)	(6.940)	(0.913)	(−1.532)		(−3.785)	
−11.032	−0.699	−0.805	−0.005	3.021	0.275	0.158	−1.151	0.037	−3.330	0.976
(−3.818)	(−1.917)	(−0.671)	(−0.486)	(8.126)	(6.221)	(1.001)	(−1.563)	(0.523)	(−3.472)	
Break and enter										
−7.410	−1.265	0.635	0.282	1.424	0.109	0.174	0.615			0.938
(−3.097)	(−5.087)	(0.651)	(1.914)	(6.633)	(3.260)	(1.788)	(1.102)			
−4.283	−0.449	−0.520	0.195	0.658	0.120	0.432	0.519	0.175		0.976
(−2.591)	(−1.956)	(−0.782)	(2.040)	(3.181)	(5.581)	(5.318)	(1.455)	(4.932)		
−7.380	−1.318	0.597	0.281	1.484	0.111	0.171	0.778		0.550	0.939
(−3.027)	(−4.951)	(0.600)	(1.872)	(6.247)	(3.227)	(1.714)	(1.252)		(0.648)	
−3.901	−0.261	−0.622	0.185	0.468	0.120	0.472	0.272	0.198	−0.791	0.979
(−2.391)	(−0.999)	(−0.957)	(1.980)	(1.912)	(5.736)	(5.600)	(0.696)	(5.144)	(−1.365)	

TABLE D.3 continued

Intercept	ln P	ln Q	ln S	ln DIST	ln VS	ln UN	ln PR	ln IND	ln A_{15-24}	R^2
Robbery										
−11.558 (−2.030)	−0.849 (−4.039)	−2.487 (−5.267)	0.353 (2.511)	0.561 (1.305)	0.180 (2.416)	−0.379 (−1.595)	1.511 (0.941)			0.944
−9.725 (−2.007)	−0.780 (−4.357)	−1.826 (−3.926)	0.280 (2.306)	0.078 (0.193)	0.178 (2.844)	0.015 (0.063)	1.325 (0.978)	0.249 (2.744)		0.962
−11.353 (−2.099)	−0.721 (−3.368)	−2.577 (−5.707)	0.298 (2.170)	0.250 (0.556)	0.154 (2.127)	−0.327 (−1.432)	0.474 (0.288)		−3.058 (−1.659)	0.952
−9.386 (−2.221)	−0.632 (−3.767)	−1.888 (−4.647)	0.214 (1.961)	−0.301 (−0.781)	0.149 (2.665)	0.098 (0.451)	0.151 (0.118)	0.264 (3.325)	−3.429 (−2.397)	0.973

NOTE: Numbers in parentheses are t-values.

TABLE D.4

Regression estimates of the offence equations, including Indian, age, and labour force activity (males aged fourteen to twenty-four) variables: ordinary least squares

Intercept	$\ln P$	$\ln Q$	$\ln S$	$\ln DIST$	$\ln VS$	$\ln UN_{14\text{-}24}$	$\ln PR_{14\text{-}24}$	$\ln IND$	$\ln A_{15\text{-}24}$	R^2
Theft A										
-4.171 (-3.310)	-0.690 (-4.698)	-0.148 (-3.000)	0.094 (1.981)	1.442 (10.196)	0.211 (10.779)	0.125 (1.692)	0.093 (0.274)			0.983
-3.181 (-3.063)	-0.650 (-5.581)	-1.360 (-3.488)	0.060 (1.564)	1.272 (10.332)	0.196 (12.054)	0.182 (3.009)	-0.032 (-0.118)	0.064 (3.274)		0.990
-4.137 (-3.162)	-0.707 (-4.216)	-1.481 (-2.916)	0.095 (1.934)	1.449 (9.764)	0.214 (9.609)	0.126 (1.652)	0.121 (0.325)		0.121 (0.227)	0.983
-3.136 (-3.137)	-0.552 (-4.236)	-1.309 (-3.479)	0.047 (1.223)	1.198 (9.332)	0.180 (9.665)	0.191 (3.242)	-0.214 (-0.741)	0.079 (3.704)	-0.662 (-1.490)	0.992
Theft B										
-4.589 (-3.705)	-0.658 (-4.149)	-1.275 (-2.648)	0.123 (2.688)	1.481 (10.767)	0.205 (10.680)	0.125 (1.701)	0.228 (0.675)			0.984
-3.626 (-3.309)	-0.662 (-4.973)	-1.157 (-2.850)	0.093 (2.334)	1.334 (10.501)	0.190 (11.284)	0.174 (2.713)	0.082 (0.284)	0.056 (2.777)		0.989
-4.590 (-3.555)	-0.657 (-3.617)	-1.275 (-2.564)	0.122 (2.585)	1.481 (10.160)	0.204 (9.563)	0.125 (1.647)	0.228 (0.622)		-0.005 (-0.009)	0.984
-3.625 (-3.391)	-0.572 (-3.899)	-1.132 (-2.853)	0.080 (2.004)	1.265 (9.403)	0.178 (9.386)	0.185 (9.929)	-0.075 (-0.246)	0.068 (3.141)	-0.598 (-1.328)	0.991

TABLE D.4 continued

Intercept	ln P	ln Q	ln S	ln DIST	ln VS	ln UN$_{14\text{-}24}$	ln PR$_{14\text{-}24}$	ln IND	ln A$_{15\text{-}24}$	R^2
Fraud										
-30.589	1.131	3.471	-0.016	3.041	0.497	0.747	4.225			0.882
(-5.691)	(2.403)	(1.594)	(-0.848)	(4.734)	(6.611)	(2.800)	(4.084)			
-26.218	1.258	3.638	-0.025	-2.654	0.492	0.818	3.462	0.101		0.883
(-2.457)	(2.284)	(1.610)	(-0.935)	(-2.548)	(6.338)	(2.633)	(1.808)	(0.478)		
-15.808	-0.839	-0.250	-0.003	3.224	0.267	0.219	0.180		-2.503	0.972
(-6.480)	(-2.777)	(-0.209)	(-0.271)	(11.797)	(5.678)	(1.638)	(0.226)		(-2.368)	
-14.633	-0.721	-0.112	-0.007	3.106	0.271	0.269	-0.071	0.042	-2.567	0.973
(-4.104)	(-1.796)	(-0.088)	(-0.515)	(8.212)	(5.527)	(1.544)	(-0.072)	(0.463)	(-2.345)	
Break and enter										
-9.889	-1.147	1.129	0.333	1.294	0.142	0.288	1.192			0.948
(-4.105)	(-4.718)	(1.213)	(2.423)	(5.942)	(4.407)	(2.646)	(2.111)			
-6.117	-0.596	-0.123	0.217	0.795	0.132	0.427	0.727	0.140		0.974
(-3.013)	(-2.592)	(-0.162)	(2.054)	(3.845)	(5.518)	(4.852)	(1.678)	(3.813)		
-9.919	-1.199	1.128	0.341	1.341	0.154	0.296	1.474		0.845	0.952
(-4.147)	(-4.876)	(1.221)	(2.495)	(6.086)	(4.561)	(2.730)	(2.394)		(1.109)	
-5.646	-0.501	-0.274	0.199	0.709	0.124	0.439	0.512	0.156	-0.474	0.975
(-2.594)	(-1.841)	(-0.341)	(1.791)	(2.897)	(4.607)	(4.809)	(0.950)	(3.513)	(-0.690)	

TABLE D.4 continued

Intercept	ln P	ln Q	ln S	ln DIST	ln VS	ln UN$_{14-24}$	ln PR$_{14-24}$	ln IND	ln A$_{15-24}$	R^2
Robbery										
-19.239	-0.780	-2.102	0.152	-0.341	0.221	0.024	3.951			0.960
(-3.972)	(-4.371)	(-5.049)	(1.206)	(-0.741)	(4.673)	(0.097)	(2.937)			
-15.331	-0.745	-1.723	0.169	-0.393	0.217	0.207	2.931	0.190		0.970
(-3.253)	(-4.617)	(-4.174)	(1.484)	(-0.948)	(5.089)	(0.878)	(2.259)	(2.181)		
-18.848	-0.724	-2.184	0.141	-0.379	0.195	0.016	3.335		-1.460	0.962
(-3.836)	(-3.761)	(-5.059)	(1.098)	(-0.811)	(3.425)	(0.834)	(0.064)		(2.157)	
-13.592	-0.629	-1.783	0.151	-0.479	0.166	0.238	1.497	0.238	-2.786	0.976
(-3.029)	(-3.855)	(-4.626)	(1.423)	(-1.231)	(3.440)	(1.083)	(1.039)	(2.795)	(-1.823)	

NOTE: Numbers in parentheses are t-values.

APPENDIX E

Data sources

This appendix lists the sources of all data used in the estimates.

The offence rate O: the number of offences recorded by the police per 1000 population. *Crime Statistics*, Statistics Canada, Cat. 85-205

The clearance rate P: the number of offences cleared by the police divided by the number of offences recorded. *Crime Statistics*, Statistics Canada, Cat. 85-205

The conviction rate Q: the number of convictions divided by the number of charges. *Statistics of Criminal and Other Offences*, Statistics Canada, Cat. 85-201. For Prince Edward Island in 1972 there were no charges for robbery and for theft, and hence no convictions. Thus, in accordance with our assumptions on the formulation of expectations, a prospective offender contemplating the commission of a robbery or theft in Prince Edward Island in 1972 would have no information on which to formulate his expectation of conviction. In these instances, previous years' values were utilized.

The length of sentence S: the number of months that a prospective offender expects to serve if convicted (see appendix A). *Statistics of Criminal and Other Offences*, Statistics Canada, Cat. 85-201 and *Correctional Institutions Statistics*, Statistics Canada, Cat. 85-207. Judicial data on sentences handed down refer to the sentence for the most serious offence for an individual during a given year. For Prince Edward Island in 1972, there were no convictions for robbery and theft, and hence, no sentences. Since the true expected sentence length is not zero, previous years' values were utilized.

The victim stock VS: the number of households with record players. *Household Facilities and Equipment*, Statistics Canada, Cat. 64-202

The total unemployment rate UN: *The Labour Force*, Statistics Canada, Cat. 71-001. Data for Prince Edward Island for 1970 and 1971 are not included. The difference of total labour force and total employment was divided by total labour force to derive the estimates for Prince Edward Island.

The total participation rate PR: *The Labour Force*, Statistics Canada, Cat. 71-001

The unemployment rate for males fourteen to twenty-four years of age UN_{14-24}: *The Labour Force*, Statistics Canada, Cat. 71-001. Data for Prince Edward Island for 1970, 1971, and 1972 were obtained by first estimating an equation between the unemployment rate for males fourteen to twenty-four and the total unemployment rate using the provincial data (excluding PEI) for the three years 1970 to 1972. The estimates were then derived using the above estimated regression coefficients and the estimated total unemployment rates for PEI.

The participation rates for males fourteen to twenty-four years of age PR_{14-24}: *The Labour Force*, Statistics Canada, Cat. 71-001

The proportion of the total male populaton aged fifteen to twenty-four A_{15-24}: *Estimated Population by Sex and Age Groups for Canada and Provinces*, Statistics Canada, Cat. 91-202, 1970 and 1972; *1971 Census of Canada, Population, Sex Ratios*, Statistics Canada, Cat. 92-714

The percentage of the total population that is North American Indian IND: *1971 Census of Canada, Population, Ethnic Groups*, Statistics Canada, Cat. 92-723

The percentage of the population living in Census Metropolitan Areas and Census Agglomeration Areas of 25,000 or more DEN: *1971 Census of Canada, Population, Sex Ratios*, Statistics Canada, Cat. 92-714

The total population POP: *Estimated Population by Sex and Age Group, For Canada and Provinces*, Statistics Canada, Cat. 91-202, 1970 and 1972; *1971 Census of Canada, Population, Sex Ratios*, Statistics Canada, Cat. 92-714

Expenditures per capita on police E: the sum of local and provincial government expenditures on police. Local government expenditures on police were provided by Statistics Canada. Provincial government expenditures on police are published in *Provincial Government Finance*, Statistics Canada, Cat. 68-207; the 1971 figures were provided in advance by Statistics Canada. The local government expenditures are on a calendar year basis, whereas the provincial government data are by fiscal year. Since it cannot be assumed that funds are disbursed evenly throughout the fiscal year, no adjustment of the fiscal year data was made.

The percentage of families that earn less than one-half the median family income DIST: *1971 Census of Canada, Summary Family Income Statistics*, Statistics Canada, Cat. 93-746. If the median income is greater than the midpoint of the income grouping, then the families within that income grouping were considered to earn incomes greater than one-half the median income.

The number of motor vehicle registrations per capita MVR: *The Motor Vehicle, Registrations*, Statistics Canada, Cat. 53-219

The total number of crimes against the person O_{PER}: *Crime Statistics*, Statistics Canada, Cat. 85-205. The variable includes the sum of murders, attempted murders, manslaughters, rapes, other sex offences, woundings, and assaults.

References

Avio, K.L. (1973) 'An economic analysis of criminal corrections: the Canadian case.' *Canadian Journal of Economics* 6, 164-78

Becker, G. (1968) 'Crime and punishment: an economic approach.' *Journal of Political Economy* 76, 169-217

Carr-Hill, R.A. and N.H. Stern (1973) 'An econometric model of the supply and control of recorded offences in England and Wales.' *Journal of Public Economics* 2, 289-318

Cassidy, R., R. Hopkinson, and W. Laycock (1973) 'Information systems report on the Canadian criminal justice system.' Ministry of State for Urban Affairs (mimeo)

Chow, G.C. (1957) *The Demand for Automobiles in the United States − A Study in Consumer Durables* (Amsterdam)

Ehrlich, I. (1973) 'Participation in illegitimate activities.' *Journal of Political Economy* 81, 521-65

Evans, R. (1973) 'Developing policies for public security and criminal justice.' Special Study No. 23, Economic Council of Canada

Fleisher, B. (1966) *The Economics of Delinquency* (Chicago: Quadrangle Books)

Goldfeld, S. and R. Quandt (1965) 'Some tests for homoskedasticity.' *Journal of American Statistical Association* 60, 539-47

Green, H.A.J. (1964) *Aggregation in Economic Analysis* (Princeton)

Greenwood, Michael J. and Walter J. Wadycki (1973) 'Crime rates and public expenditures for police protection: their interaction.' *Review of Social Economy* 31, 138-51

Henderson, J. and R. Quandt (1971) *Microeconomic Theory* (New York: McGraw-Hill)

Hogarth, J. (1967) 'Towards the improvement of sentencing in Canada.' *Canadian Journal of Corrections* 9, 122-36

Reynolds, M. (1971) 'Crimes for profit: the economics of theft.' PhD dissertation, University of Wisconsin

Sjoquist, D. (1973) 'Property crime and economic behavior: some empirical results.' *American Economic Review* 63, 439-46

Statistics Canada Publications: see appendix E

Swimmer, E. (1974) 'Measurement of the effectiveness of urban law enforcement – a simultaneous approach.' *Southern Economic Journal* 40, 618-30

Theil, H. (1954) *Linear Aggregation of Economic Relations* (Amsterdam)

Tobin, J. (1950) 'A statistical demand function for food in the USA' *Journal of the Royal Statistical Society* Series A, 113-49

Tullock, G. (1969) 'An economic approach to crime.' *Social Science Quarterly* 50, 59-71

- (1974) 'Does punishment deter crime?' *Public Interest* 36, 103-11

Uniform Crime Reporting Manual (1974) Judicial Division, Statistics Canada (Ottawa)

9 780802 033345